The Oxford Student's Harmony

A PRACTICAL APPROACH TO
CREATIVE MUSICIANSHIP

EDWIN SMITH
and
DAVID RENOUF

BOOK ONE

Music Department
OXFORD UNIVERSITY PRESS
WALTON STREET, OXFORD OX2 6DP

Oxford University Press, Walton Street, Oxford OX2 6DP
Oxford New York Toronto
Delhi Bombay Calcutta Madras Karachi
Kuala Lumpur Singapore Hong Kong Tokyo
Nairobi Dar es Salaam Cape Town
Melbourne Auckland
and associated companies in
Beirut Berlin Ibadan Nicosia

OXFORD *is a trade mark of Oxford University Press*

© *Oxford University Press 1965*
First published 1965
Ninth impression 1986

All rights reserved. No part of this publication may be reproduced, performed, stored in a retrieval system, or transmitted, in any form or by any means, electronic, mechanical, photocopying, recording, or otherwise, without the prior permission of Oxford University Press or the appropriate licensing authority

This book is sold subject to the condition that it shall not, by way of trade or otherwise, be lent, re-sold, hired out, or otherwise circulated without the publisher's prior consent in any form of binding or cover other than that in which it is published and without a similar condition including this condition being imposed on the subsequent purchaser

ISBN 019 321631 0

Reproduced and printed by
Halstan & Co. Ltd., Amersham, Bucks., England

INTRODUCTION

The need for artistic creativity in education is well understood, but its importance at the present time can hardly be over-stated. Our society grows daily more complex and industrialized, and along with the benefits of science and technology come the problems that are their counterpart. If we are not to be overwhelmed by traffic, noise, bureaucracy, and the trivialities of mass media—to mention but a few of the problems that beset us—we shall certainly need to do everything possible in education to nurture the individual and help him develop his innate powers and resources. Only a community valuing personal development and integrity and respecting art and culture will be able to combat the dehumanizing forces of modern urban life.

Music has an important part to play in the establishment of such a community. In recent years creative work has begun to figure more prominently in class music teaching, especially at the primary stage. Increasing use is being made of instruments. Just as children experiment with a variety of media in art and craft, acquiring skill and control through the handling of materials, in a similar way we now find children experimenting more and more with instruments and sounds and experiencing the joy that comes from creating music individually and in groups.

Unfortunately, these early explorations are not always followed up in any significant way in later musical training. The study of harmony, in particular, is often a drab affair. A preoccupation with the demands of public examinations and an over-emphasis on 'rules' and prohibitions give rise to an arid approach where theory is divorced from practice, imagination is stifled, and a good deal of native talent goes unrealized. There can be little justification for the study of harmony if it does not result in creative expression. Not all students will become professional musicians but, whatever their eventual occupation, they should all be composers to some extent, and from the outset a successful harmony course should evoke compositions as profuse and satisfying in their way as the paintings and sketches of the student artist.

These books have been planned to encourage a practical and creative approach in colleges and schools where harmony is studied in class. They aim to establish fundamental concepts in harmony and style and to provide for the enjoyable acquisition of skill in improvisation, sight-reading, harmonization, and transposition.

Principles of melody and harmony are exemplified in quotations from acknowledged composers and from folk music. Each example should be carefully studied and rehearsed in an endeavour to appreciate to the full its peculiar style and character. It is essential that students be provided with regular opportunities to perform singly and in groups and to conduct rehearsals. They should attempt as many as possible of the various projects suggested and prepare performances for the class. We cannot too strongly urge that each student's work be performed in this way and that the teacher and members of the class listen carefully and contribute constructive criticisms.

We hope that the many quotations will whet the student's appetite, arousing a desire to know more about the works from which they are taken and setting him off on a life-long exploration of the scores of the great masters. We hope too that they will fire his imagination and inspire him to develop his own powers of expression.

Acknowledgements are due to the following for permission to reproduce extracts from songs or music: Boosey and Hawkes Ltd. (Delius's *Appalachia*, Weinberger's *Schwanda the Bagpiper*, Prokoviev's *Classical Symphony*); G. Schirmer Inc. (Chappell and Co., London) (Menotti's *Amahl and the Night Visitors*); J. B. Cramer and Co. Ltd. ('As I Sat on a Sunny Bank' and 'The Tree in the Valley' from *English County Songs*); J. Curwen and Sons Ltd. ('Old Farmer Buck' from *Community Song Book*, 'Sweet Nightingale', 'The Drummer and the Cook', 'Billy Boy', and 'Carrion Crow'); Durand et Cie., Paris (Ravel's *Ma mère l'Oye*); The English Folk Song and Dance Society ('The Steamboat', 'The De'il Among the Tailors', and 'The Irish Washerwoman' from *Fiddler's Tune Book*); Galliard Ltd. (Holst's setting of Psalm 148); Novello and Co. Ltd. ('The Lark in the Morn' and 'As I walked through the Meadows' from *A Selection of Collected Folk Songs*, 'The Deaf Woman's Courtship' and 'Go and Tell Aunt Nancy' from *Seventeen Nursery Songs from the Appalachian Mountains*, and German's incidental music from *Henry VIII*); Schott and Co. Ltd. (Humperdinck's *Hansel and Gretel*, Tippett's *A Child of Our Time*, and 'The Dead Horse' from *English Folk Chanteys*); Stainer and Bell Ltd. ('On Christmas Night' from *Eight Traditional Christmas Carols*, arr. Vaughan Williams); Universal Edition (London) Ltd. (Kodály's *Háry János*); David S. McIntosh ('Roll That Brown Jug'); Oxford University Press (Walton's *Belshazzar's Feast*, Vaughan Williams's *The Lark Ascending*, 'Joseph Dearest' from *Oxford Book of Carols*, 'O Where are you Going Sally Anne' from *Twelve Songs for Children*, 'All through the Night' from *Songs of Praise*, and songs from *Oxford School Music Books*).

CONTENTS

INTRODUCTION

			Page
CHAPTER 1	MELODY	Balancing phrases: statement and response	1
	HARMONY	The tonic and dominant chords in root position	2
		Perfect and imperfect cadences	9
		Passing and auxiliary notes	11
2	MELODY	Balancing phrases continued	13
	HARMONY	The tonic and dominant chords and their first inversions	14
3	MELODY	Setting words to music	22
	HARMONY	The dominant seventh chord in root position	27
4	MELODY	Passing and auxiliary notes	41
	HARMONY	The dominant and supertonic sevenths and their inversions	47
5	HARMONY	The subdominant chord	63
		The plagal cadence	66
	MELODY	The pentatonic scale	67
6	HARMONY	The appoggiatura	75
		The cadential six-four chord	77
7	HARMONY	The mediant and submediant chords	87
		The interrupted cadence	91
		The dominant thirteenth	92
8	INSTRUMENTAL WRITING	Arranging for recorders and percussion	100
	VOCAL WRITING	Two-part writing	109
		Three and four-part writing	115
		Solo, chorus and accompaniment	130

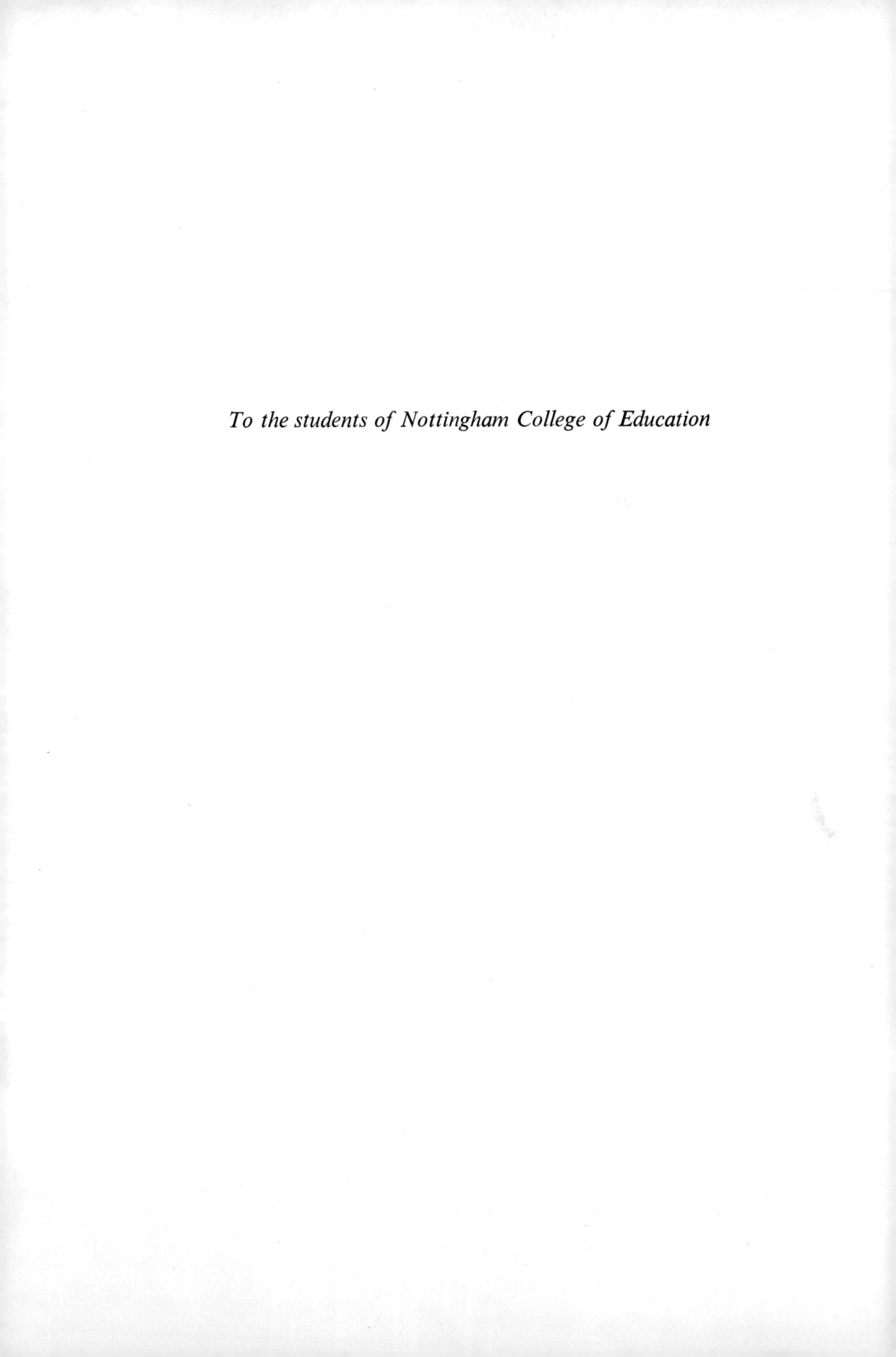

To the students of Nottingham College of Education

CHAPTER ONE

MELODY

Countless melodies consist of two phrases, statement and response:

The statement sounds incomplete by itself. It is balanced by the response. The two phrases together make up a complete musical sentence.

Sing and play *soh* and *doh* at * in the following sentences.

1. Brightly

2. With a swing

3. Sadly

Sing and play responses to the following statements.

4. Briskly

5. Gracefully

mp s d*

6. Sturdily

f s d

Sing, play and write sentences of your own invention in the following styles: cheerful; thoughtful; martial; pastoral; angry; lilting; jerky.

HARMONY

We have noticed the importance of the 1st and 5th notes of the scale (*doh* and *soh*).*

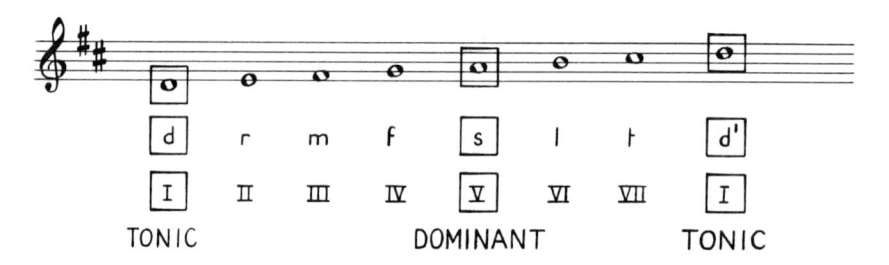

d	r	m	f	s	l	t	d'
I	II	III	IV	V	VI	VII	I
TONIC				DOMINANT			TONIC

If we sing above them notes at intervals of a third and fifth, we have major triads ('major' because the lowest interval is a major third, and 'triad' because the chords are of three notes).

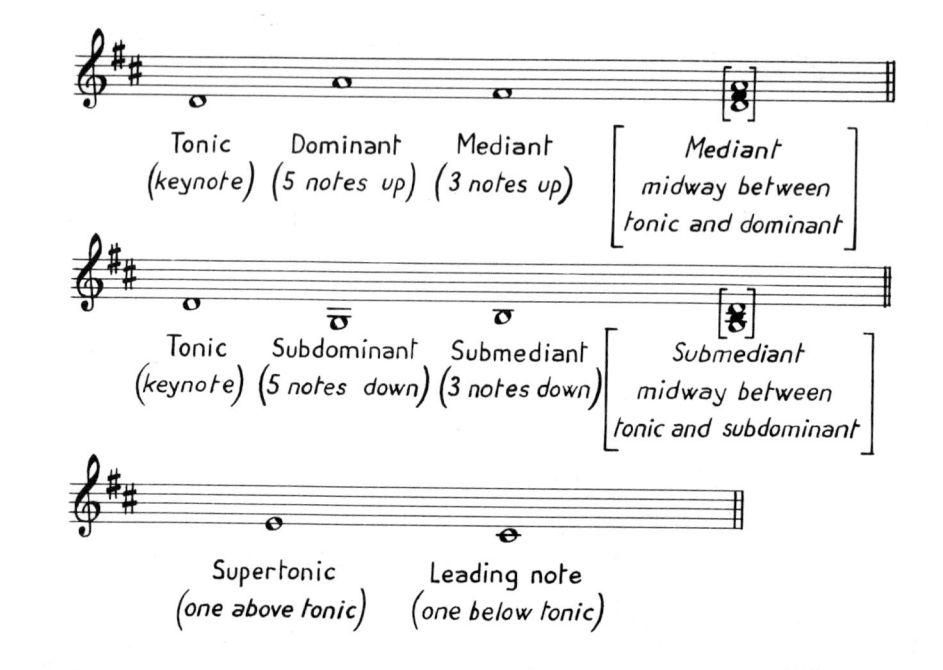

---

*

Tonic   Dominant   Mediant   [Mediant
(keynote)   (5 notes up) (3 notes up)   midway between
                                            tonic and dominant]

Tonic   Subdominant   Submediant   [Submediant
(keynote)   (5 notes down) (3 notes down)   midway between
                                            tonic and subdominant]

Supertonic   Leading note
(one above tonic)   (one below tonic)

[Musical notation: In D major, "Sing" d m s, then "Play" Root Third Fifth — doh chord]

Root Third Fifth — doh chord
(Tonic) (Mediant) (Dominant) (otherwise Tonic chord)
(or just I)

[Musical notation: In D major, "Sing" s t r¹, then "Play" Root Third Fifth — soh chord]

Root Third Fifth — soh chord
(Dominant) (Leading-note) (Supertonic) (otherwise Dominant chord, or just V)

Find the tonic chord in the key of D major in various parts of the piano, e.g.:

Similarly, find five examples of the tonic chord in each of the following keys: C, G, A, F, B flat, E flat.

Find the dominant chord in the key of D major in five different parts of the keyboard, e.g.:

Similarly, find the dominant chord in the keys of C, G, A, F, B flat, and E flat.

By distributing the notes of the triad over a wide range, and by doubling or omitting some of them, different effects may be obtained. Play these arrangements of the tonic chord in C major and listen carefully to the results:

[Musical example with labels: Bright (a), Full (b), Heavy (c), Solid (d), Gruff (e), Very bright (f), Grand (g), Hollow (h), Impressive (j)]

Notice:
    (1) Doubling the root (a, b, c, e, f)
    (2) Trebling the root (h, j)
    (3) Quadrupling the root (d)
    (4) Doubling the third (f, g)
    (5) Omitting the third (h, j)
    (6) Doubling the fifth (g)
    (7) Trebling the fifth (j)
    (8) Grouping deep bass notes close together (e)
    (9) Spreading bass notes (d, f, g, h, j)

Comment on these arrangements of the tonic chord in the key of G, and say what effect each produces:

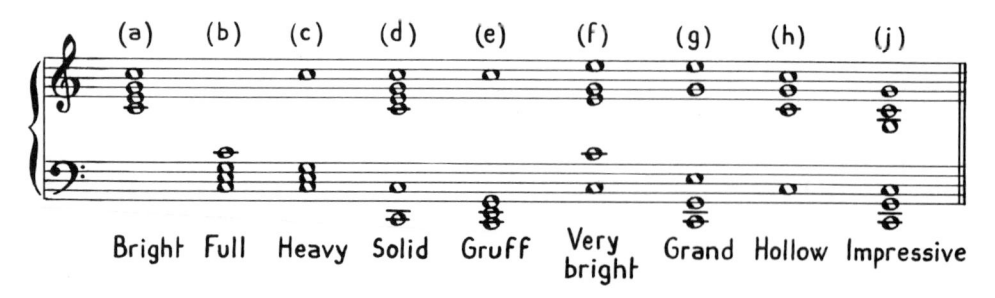

[Musical example with arrangements labeled (a) through (g)]

Notice that:
    Doubling the root or fifth gives extra strength and weight to a chord.
    Doubling the third gives extra brightness and should therefore be used when such an effect is needed rather than as common practice.
    Omitting the fifth takes some of the fullness from a chord.
    Omitting the third leaves arrangements that may lack warmth yet gain in dignity.
    Notes crowded together in the bass give a thick, heavy effect.
    Notes crowded together in the treble help to avoid the effect of thinness which high notes tend to produce.

Make further experiments with different arrangements of chords in various keys.

    Turn back to page 1 and fit dominant and tonic chords in the appropriate places, e.g.,

Sing the melodies and *play* the chords.
  Sing this extract (*O.S.M.B. Beginners*, Pupil's Book I, page 8).

There were ten in the bed and the little one said, 'Roll o-ver! Roll o-ver!'

Notice that all the notes belong to the tonic chord in G major.
  Sing the extract again, this time to the tonic sol-fa syllables.

s₁ s₁ d d d d s₁ s₁ d d d d s m d s m d

We will now devise an easy accompaniment based entirely upon the tonic chord.
  Sing and play twice.

d' s m d d' d d' d

Sing and play again, but this time from memory.
  Play this, still singing the bass to sol-fa syllables:

[Musical notation with solfa: d' s m d d' d d' d]

Now sing the song and accompany yourself.

Briskly

[Musical notation with lyrics: There were ten in the bed and the little one said, 'Roll o-ver! Roll o-ver!']

Sing the song and accompany yourself again, but *from memory*.

Now do the same but in the keys of F, A, B flat, A flat, E. (It is just as easy in the key of F sharp—all black notes.)

Devise an accompaniment, based upon the tonic and dominant chords, to 'Hark, the Posthorn' (*O.S.M.B. Beginners*, Pupil's Book II, page 4).

Try this in several other keys too.

In lively style

[Musical notation with lyrics: Hark, the post-horn! Here comes the Roy-al Mail, Hark, the post-horn! Here comes the Mail. O-ver the hills and on Rides the pos-til-li-on, O-ver hills and down the dale.]

Choose a member of your group to rehearse the following round. We will leave him to decide the gradations of dynamics that will evoke a realistic imitation of the horn.

[Musical example: "The huntsman's sounding his horn there, So loud and gay, He's galloping swift through the thorn there, The hunt's away." marked Vivace, Trad.]

The notes at the beginning of the first bar are those of the dominant chord; those of the second bar, the tonic chord.

[Musical example: V–I progression in B flat]

Here we have an example of a simple harmonic progression (the name given to a succession of chords). When we come to write our own progressions, we have not only to choose chords that sound well in succession, we have also to consider the way in which the individual parts move as the chords are connected. Our first aim must be to write smooth progressions.

In a progression involving two root-position chords, this smoothness is usually achieved in four-part writing by ensuring that the three upper parts move as little as possible. Where a note is common to both triads it is repeated in the same part. The other two parts move from their notes in one triad to the nearest note in the next.

In the progression V–I, this will usually mean that the dominant will be repeated in the same voice; the leading note will rise to the tonic, and the supertonic will rise to the mediant. On occasions when the supertonic falls one degree to the tonic, it is customary for the dominant not to be repeated, but to fall to the mediant.

Here are a number of arrangements of chords V–I in the key of B flat in which these points are illustrated:

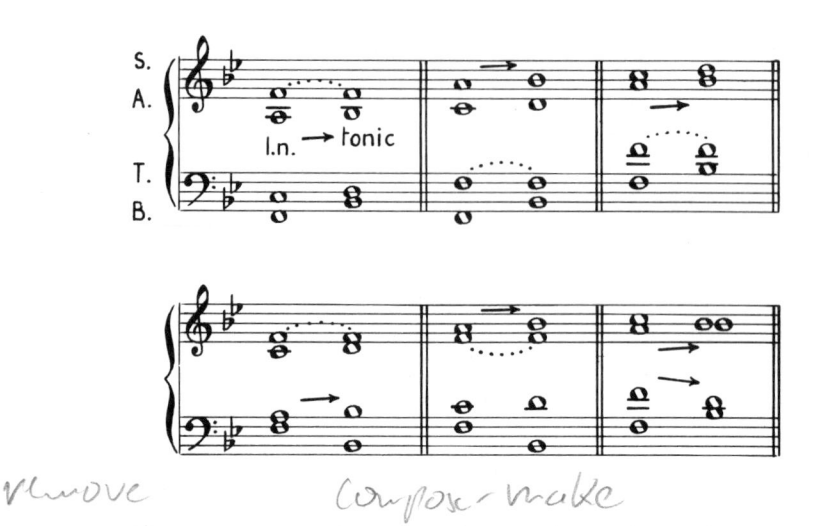

Let us now return to our round and treat it as though it were a unison song. We delete the pauses and devise a piano accompaniment. We decide that where there are few quavers in the melody we will provide some movement in the accompaniment by the use of broken chords, bearing in mind the points mentioned in the discussion on part-movement in the previous paragraph.

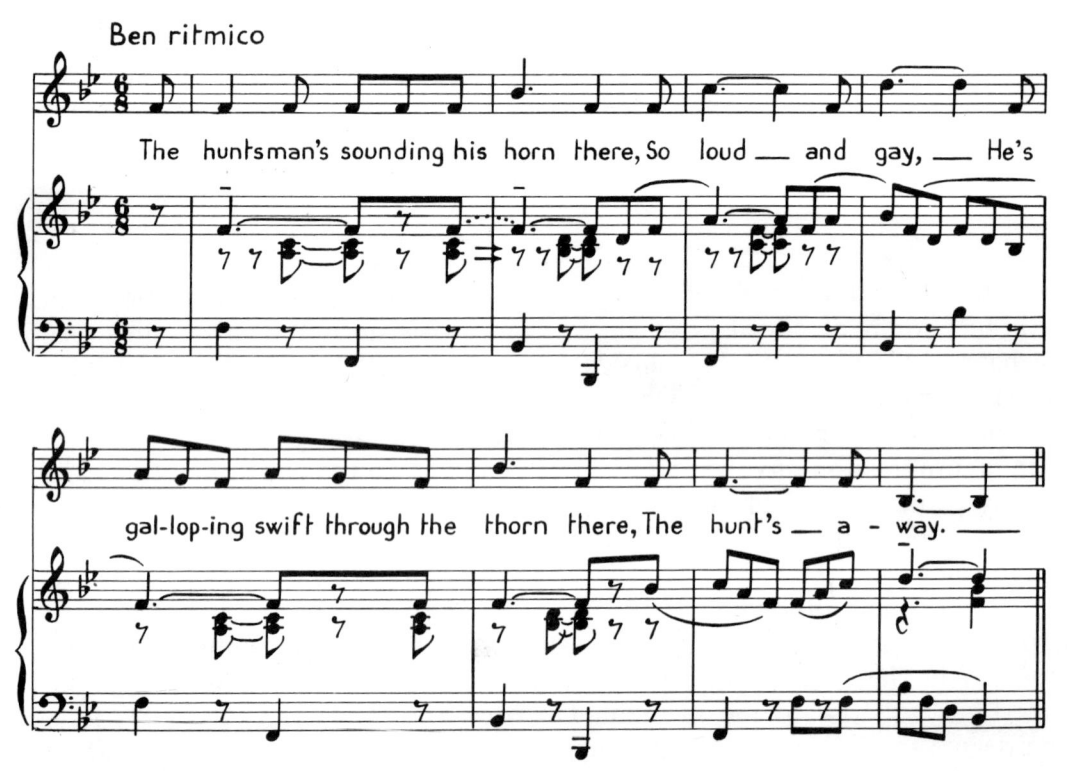

Write an accompaniment for this Czech folk-song. Give a performance to your group.

The Little Butcher

Allegretto

A¹ What's the matter with our butcher? What can he be doing?
(I ... V)

A² He is out again with Anna, he has gone a-wooing.
(I ... V I)

B Does he want to hold her tight? Will he kiss her? Yes, he might!
(I V I V)

A³ Off they go like lovey doves, a-billing and a-cooing.
(I ... V I)

This melody has four phrases—AABA. In the A music there are three consecutive bars of tonic harmony, whereas in the B music tonic and dominant alternate. A¹ and A² together make a complete sentence, A¹ ending on the dominant, and A² on the tonic. Similarly, B and A³ are the statement and response of a second musical sentence. The B music is based upon the last two bars of A¹.

When a phrase ends with the chords V–I, we have a PERFECT CADENCE (a musical full stop).

When a phrase ends on V, we have an IMPERFECT CADENCE (a musical comma) or HALF CLOSE.

Say which phrases end with perfect and which with imperfect cadences in the above two songs.

Add soprano, alto, and tenor to these bass parts:

PERFECT CADENCES
(i) V I
(ii)
(iii)

IMPERFECT CADENCES
(iv) I V
(v)
(vi)

Add alto, tenor, and bass to these soprano parts:
PERFECT CADENCES

IMPERFECT CADENCES

Sing the following phrase which is taken from a folk-song, 'The Lark in the Morn'.

Did you notice that the tune is based on the triad of G?

In other words, the tune suggests the harmony that may be used to accompany it. Let one member of your group sing the melody while the others sustain a quiet chord of G major as follows:

The notes marked * are known as PASSING NOTES. They fill in the gaps as we pass from one note of a triad to another, and the result is a passage that rises or falls by steps (conjunct movement). Since passing notes are foreign to the triads that they decorate they are known as UNESSENTIAL NOTES.

Here is another phrase that is based on the chord of G:

[Musical notation: Moderato, mp, German Carol — "Jo-seph dear-est, Jo-seph mine, Help me cradle the child di-vine."]

Here we meet a different kind of unessential note, namely, the AUXILIARY NOTE*. This is a note one tone or one semitone above or below a harmony note. It is heard between two soundings of the harmony note.

Again we will sing a quiet accompaniment, but this time we will use both tonic and dominant chords:

[Musical notation: SSA with Solo — "Jo-seph dear-est, Jo-seph mine, Help me cradle the child di-vine."]

At the beginning of *Das Rheingold*, the first of Wagner's four operas which comprise *The Ring*, there are 136 bars based entirely on the chord of E flat major. Study the vocal score and try to hear a recording of the opening scene, and you will discover what wonderful music can be evolved from a single chord embroidered with passing notes. Here is a quotation from that same scene. The music has moved into C major. The three Rhine-maidens who guard the magic gold embedded in a rock jutting out of the river, are singing and sporting as they swim around the rock which glows with a brilliant golden light.

Sing and play this extract. Look for the passing and auxiliary notes and note their effect.

12　　Joyfully　　　　　　　　　　　　　　　　　　Wagner, Das Rheingold

S: Hei-a ja-hei-a! Hei-a ja-hei-a! Wal-la-la la la la lei-a ja- hei!

S: Hei-a ja-hei-a! Hei-a ja-hei-a! Wal-la-la la la la lei-a ja- hei!

A: Hei-a ja-hei-a! Hei-a ja-hei-a! Wal-la-la la la lei-a ja- hei!

Piano

The following quotations are from famous musical works. Try to hear each one in your mind; then sing it; finally play it.

Moderato　　　　　　　　　　　　　　　Suppé, Light Cavalry Overture

Andante　　　　　　　　　　　　　　　　　Delius, Appalachia

Briskly　　　　　　　　　　　　　　　　　　Bizet, Carmen

Allegro vivace　　　　　　　　　　Schubert, Symphony in C (The Great)

These four themes are based exclusively upon the notes of the tonic chord, yet their styles are contrasted, due to their differing tempi, rhythms, dynamics, instrumentation, etc.

Whenever possible, listen to recordings and study the scores of the compositions from which we quote.

CHAPTER TWO

MELODY

In Chapter One, our melodies consisted of two balancing phrases, in which the statement ended on *s* and the response on *d*. You practised fitting the dominant chord at the end of the statement, and the tonic chord at the end of the response.

Now since there are three notes in a triad, your first phrase might very well have ended on *r* or *t*, and the balancing phrase on *m* or *s*.

Sing and play the following tunes. At the end of each statement try the effect of *r*, *t*, and *s* in turn and see which you prefer. Similarly, try the effect of *d*, *m*, or *s* at the end of the response. The supertonic is a good note on which to end an opening phrase. It suggests that the music must flow forward, and 'flow' is an essential quality in music. A beautiful effect may be obtained by ending a melody on *m* or *s*. Much depends, of course, on the mood of the melody and its tempo and dynamics. Notice particularly the effect of *m* at the end of a slow melody. It gives a feeling of tranquillity and is less 'final' than the tonic.

Complete the following sentences:

14

[Clar. 3. in B♭ — Allegro sostenuto, mf]

[Horn 4. in F — Poco allegretto, mf]

The clarinet and horn are transposing instruments. When the player plays C on a B flat clarinet, it sounds B flat, one tone lower than the printed note. Similarly, when C is played on a horn in F, F is sounded, a perfect fifth lower. Practise playing your melodies at the sounding pitch.

HARMONY

When the lowest sounding note of a chord is the root, then the chord is said to be in root position. But when the notes of a triad are so arranged that the third or the fifth becomes the lowest sounding note, then the chord is said to have been inverted.

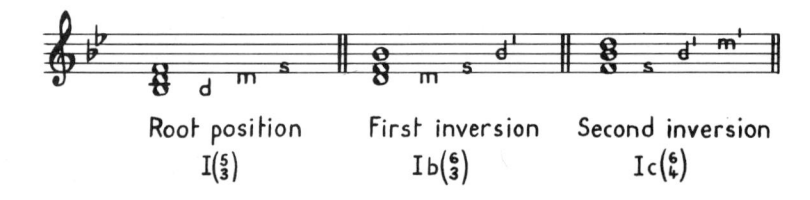

Root position   First inversion   Second inversion
I($^5_3$)   Ib($^6_3$)   Ic($^6_4$)

For the present we shall deal only with the root positions and first inversions of chords I and V.

Sing   Play   Sing   Play

Root position   d m s   First inversion   m s d'

Here is a three-part round. Vary the method of performance. After singing it as set, sing it to sol-fa names, hum it, and sing it to 'lah'.

Moderato

1. O what a plea-sure, Bliss beyond measure, Just to sing the to-nic chord.
2. Pitch it pure-ly, Time it tru-ly, O-ver-tones will then be heard.
3. Root po-si-tion, First in-ver-sion, Last, a chord with-out a third.

Play these arrangements of chord Ib in key B flat, and consider their various effects:

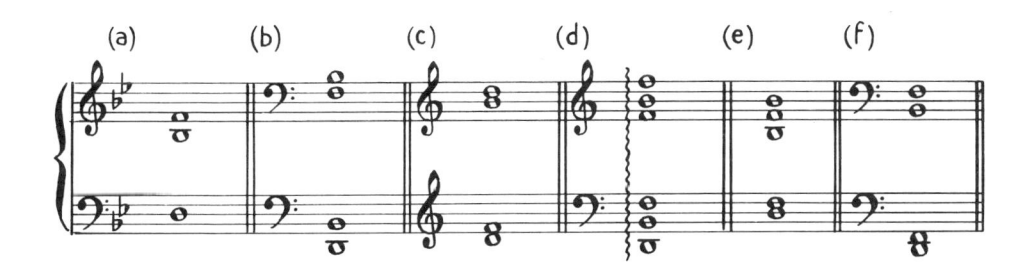

(a) (b) (c) (d) (e) (f)

First inversions have less solidity than root position chords. Did you feel this lighter quality?

Experiment for yourself. Play at least six arrangements of Vb in key B flat. Keep in mind the suggestions made in Chapter One about spacing and doubling. Remember that what was said about the third of the root position chord now applies to the bass of the first inversion, the fifth has become a third above the bass, and the root a sixth above the bass.

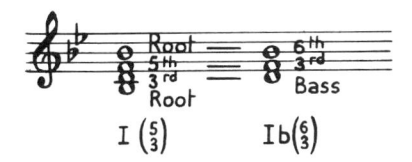

$I \begin{pmatrix} 5 \\ 3 \end{pmatrix}$ $Ib \begin{pmatrix} 6 \\ 3 \end{pmatrix}$

Sing and play the following:

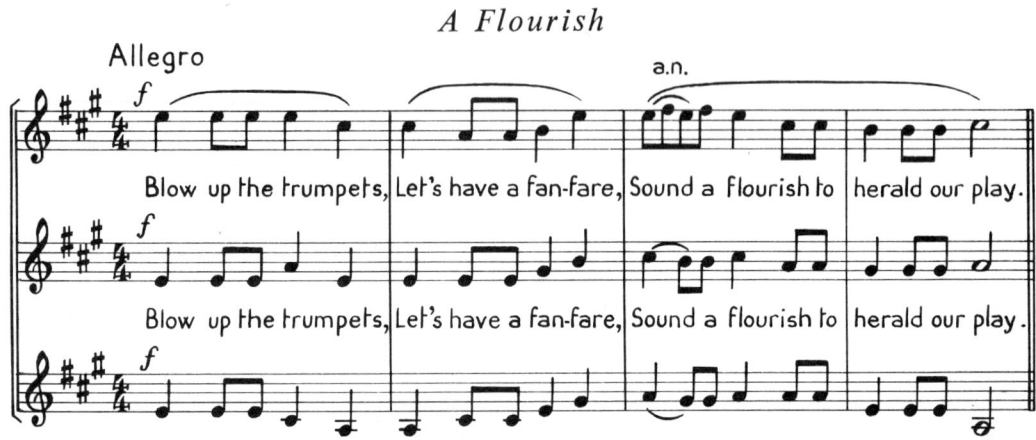

A Flourish

[Musical score: Allegro, three vocal parts in A major, 2/4 time, with lyrics "Blow up the trumpets, Let's have a fan-fare, Sound a flourish to herald our play." marked *f* with "a.n." notation]

This passage demonstrates two important uses of the first inversion.

1. When a single harmony is employed for a number of beats (or possibly bars), by moving from root position to first inversion, and vice versa, we introduce movement into the bass part, making it more flexible and melodious. Very often this movement in the bass coincides with movement in the melody. Our 'Flourish' shows the three forms such movement usually takes:

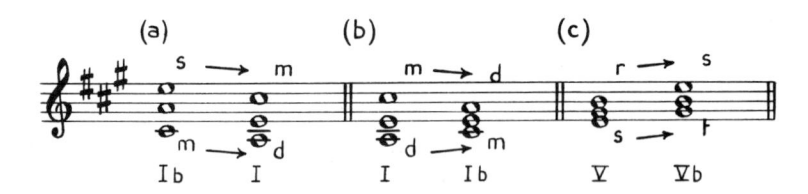

[Musical examples labeled (a), (b), (c) showing chord progressions: (a) Ib → I with s→m and m→d; (b) I → Ib with m→d and d→m; (c) V → Vb with r→s and s→f]

In (a) and (c) the three parts move in the same direction from one position of the chord to another. We say that they move in similar motion. In (b), the melody and bass move in contrary motion. Because of this independent part-movement we get a stronger effect.

These progressions may all be reversed:

[Musical examples labeled (d), (e), (f) showing reversed chord progressions]

There are occasions, of course, when the bass moves but the melody does not (oblique motion):

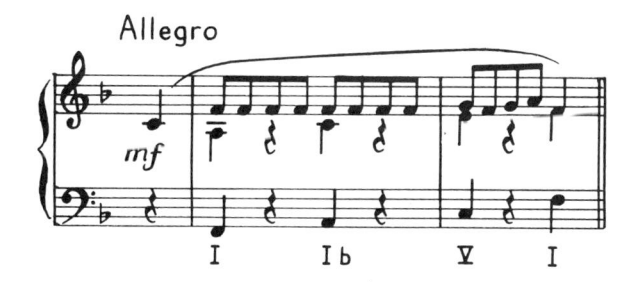

[Musical example: Allegro, with chord labels I, Ib, V, I]

2. By using first inversions along with root positions it becomes possible to get step-wise movement in the bass part. Within the limits of our present resources this will only occur in progressions involving chords I and Vb:

[Musical example with chord labels I, Vb, I]

You are advised to play the 'Flourish' many times and in a number of keys, until you are really familiar with the sound of the various progressions.

Purcell's 'Trumpet Tune' is also built upon chords I and V and their first inversions. Memorize this too. Sing the bass to sol-fa names as you play.

[Musical example: Maestoso, f]

We will now harmonize a folk-song, using chords I, Ib, V, and Vb.

[Musical example: Semplice, p]

1. In this Appalachian cradle-song there are two balancing phrases, and the first one ends on the dominant. We therefore decide that the first phrase should end with chord V and the response with chord I.

2. We notice that chord I will be required for the whole of the first two bars. In other words, the harmonies do not change frequently, and we decide that our harmonic rhythm will be:

3. The second phrase calls for fewer decisions than the first one, so it will help if we harmonize this phrase first. Since most pieces of music end firmly with two root position chords, we decide to end in the normal way with V–I in root position. The most suitable place for a first inversion is the second bar of the phrase. Our bass will therefore be:

4. We have now to consider the various possibilities in phrase one, and to select a bass which will be shapely and flowing, leading naturally into the second phrase, and having a touch of variety if possible. Here are a number of possibilities. Try them in turn against the tune. Which one do you prefer?

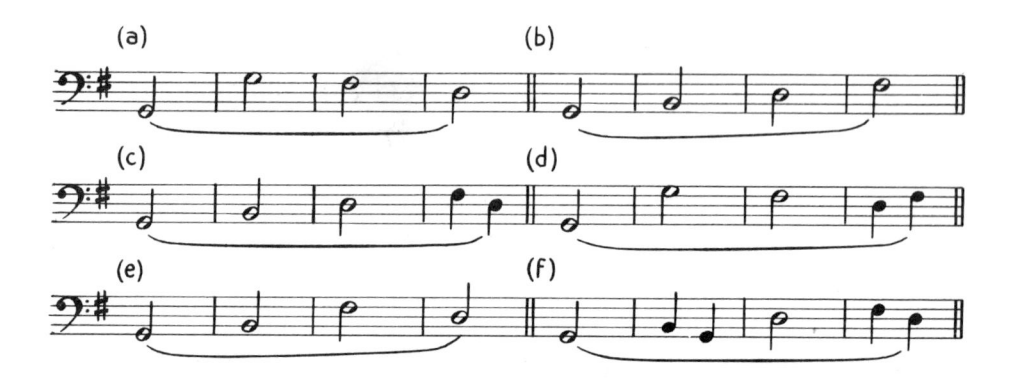

When there is a long note in the tune, it is often desirable to have shorter notes in the accompaniment. This helps to keep the music flowing onwards, and is especially effective in linking one phrase to another.

Suppose we select the version at (c).

Finally we add an inner part to produce the warmer effect of a simple three-part arrangement.

Here are five more melodies to be harmonized in a similar way. Decide upon the dynamics yourselves.

Play these progressions in all the major keys:

In four-part harmony it is better not to double the bass of a major first inversion unless there is some good reason for doing so.

Consider the effect of the following:

Chords (ii) and (iii) are less clear in sound than chord (i). Chord (iii) is the least satisfactory because the doubled bass note occurs among the upper parts.

But remember that we are discussing a chord in isolation. Consider the effect of this chord in a musical context. You will find it in the first bar of the Purcell 'Trumpet Tune' on page 17. Here it sounds well because of the melodic nature of the bass part. Doubled major thirds are not uncommon in music, but when they occur they usually arise as a result of interesting part movement. Here are two examples. Find other examples for yourself and discuss them with your group.

Harmonize the following for SATB using chords I, Ib, V, and Vb. Add phrasing and expression marks and decide on suitable tempi.

Here are further quotations based on the tonic chord. Play them and say which notes are harmony notes, which are passing notes, and which are auxiliary notes.

Say whether you prefer tonic harmony throughout the following extracts. In which bars might dominant harmony be appropriate?

CHAPTER THREE

MELODY

Setting Words to Music
Metre is one of the features that verse and music have in common. Not all verse is metrical, but in most of the poetry written before the present century there is an underlying, regular pulsation produced by an ordered arrangement of strong and weak accents.

The unit of poetic metre is the foot, corresponding to the bar in music, and just as there are different measures in music, so there are different metres in verse. Here are three such metres. Each one has been reproduced in musical notation, but there are other ways in which this might have been done as we shall see later.

IAMBIC ‿ —   I saw three ships come sail-ing in

TROCHAIC — ‿   Gol-den slum-bers kiss your eyes

DACTYLIC — ‿ ‿   Sing me a song of a lad that is gone

When we read poetry we are conscious of the underlying metrical pattern, but this does not govern the manner of our delivery; we make no attempt to put an equal stress on each strong beat of the metre. To do so would result in a 'sing-song' performance that would be quite inartistic. Instead, we adopt a speech-rhythm; we arrange our stresses and quantities in the way best calculated to bring out the poet's thought and feeling.

Sometimes the accents of speech-rhythm coincide with the accents of the metre; quite often the two are out of step. Much of our pleasure in poetry arises from an awareness of the rhythmic counterpoint that emerges when the accents of a flexible speech-rhythm conflict with the accents of a regular metre. The amount of such rhythmic interplay varies from poem to poem and within the same poem. But there is usually a large measure of agreement between the two kinds of accents in nursery rhymes, carols, ballads and short lyrical poems, especially those written for singing, and those intended as an accompaniment to dancing. For the present we shall confine our attention to this type of verse.

In setting such verse to music there will be no difficulty in finding a rhythmic pattern to match the poetic metre. On the contrary, there is a danger that we may be beguiled by the incantatory nature of the metre into producing a rhythm that is too repetitive and monotonous. We must guard against this. A simple poem requires a simple setting, but there is no reason why our rhythm should not preserve the lilt of the poem and yet have a measure of independence and flexibility.

With these points in mind, let us return to the three examples quoted above and see what we can learn from them. In the first example we find the iambic metre with its alternation of weak and strong accents. Since this arrangement of pulses occurs in many musical measures the metre may be notated in a variety of ways. Here are three possibilities:

Here is the carol in its traditional setting:

The regular, lilting metre reminds us that carols originated in the dance. Although the rhythm is repetitive and syllabic (one note to one syllable), nevertheless, we feel that it is the right one for this carol. It evokes the spirit of the dance and suits the simplicity of the verses. A setting in $\frac{2}{4}$ time would be far too staid and hymn-like. $\frac{3}{4}$ time would be better, but would still fail to suggest the right kind of spring and gaiety. We decide that $\frac{6}{8}$ is the most appropriate measure for these particular verses.

Our next example is a gentle, flowing lullaby.

[Musical notation: "Golden slumbers kiss your eyes, Smiles awake you when you rise; Sleep pretty maiden, do not cry, And I will sing a lullaby."]

Notice that this setting is not entirely syllabic. When a number of notes are sung to one syllable, such a group is called a melisma. Much of the beauty of this melody arises from the happy blend of syllabic and melismatic treatment. Notice the third phrase particularly. There is a slight increase of tension here produced by the crotchet movement, the rise and fall of the melody, and the appoggiatura* on the word 'cry'. This gentle climax comes at the right point, psychologically. It enhances the beauty of the final phrase.

Remember then that the melisma will help you to get variety into your rhythms, and will often be invaluable in word-painting.

Here are two fine examples:

[Musical notation: Allegro moderato — Handel, Judas Maccabaeus — "And valleys smile with wavy corn"]

[Musical notation: Tempo di marcia energica — Walton, Belshazzar's Feast — "Praise ye the god of iron"]

So far we have dealt solely with matters of rhythm. When you come to set words to music, you will find, with experience, that rhythm and pitch tend to come to mind together; but in your early attempts you are advised to make rhythm your first consideration. Once you have found a satisfactory rhythm a tune will soon take shape.

Let us put these suggestions into practice. We will set the following verses:

---

* See Chapter Six for a fuller explanation of the appoggiatura.

> As we dance round a-ring-a-ring,
> A maiden goes a-maying;
> And here a flower, and there a flower,
> Through mead and meadow straying:
> O gentle one, why dost thou weep?—
> Silver to spend with; gold to keep;
> Till spin the green round world asleep,
> And heaven its dews be staying.

Here we have a dance-song. The words are old and have a strong, lilting iambic metre. Notice where the accents of speech-rhythm occur in lines five, six and seven. The slight changes of rhythm here give a beautiful effect. We realise that we shall be able to get variety and avoid undue repetition.

We will now mark the accented syllables of speech-rhythm. We next examine a regular line such as line three. As we recite this line we realise that the accents on 'here' and 'there' are stronger than those on 'flower'. If we beat time as we recite we find ourselves beating two-in-a-bar. We can now draw in our bar-lines, placing them before the strong accents.

> Ās we dance rōund a|rīng-a-rīng,
> A |maiden gōes a|māying;
> And |hēre a flōwer, and |thēre a flōwer,
> Through |mēad and meadow |strāying:
> O |gēntle ōne, |whȳ dost thou wēep?—
> |Sīlver to spēnd with; |gōld to kēep;
> Till |spīn the grēen round |wōrld aslēep,
> And |hēaven its dēws be |stāying.

Since it is a dance-song we will adopt the $\frac{6}{8}$ metre. Our setting will be mainly syllabic in order to suggest the dance, but we will introduce a number of melismas, partly to get variety, but chiefly to give a pastoral effect, and to convey the idea of 'straying'.

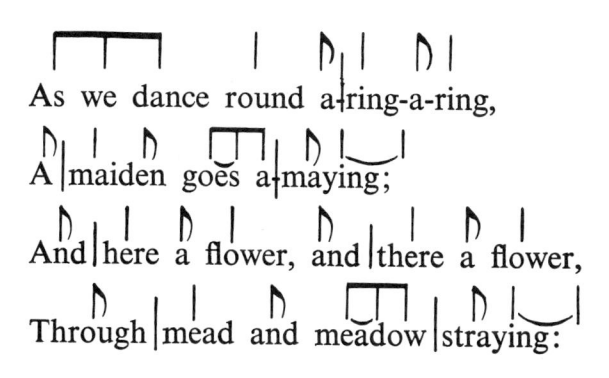

O gentle one, why dost thou weep?
Silver to spend with; gold to keep;
Till spin the green round world asleep,
And heaven its dews be staying.

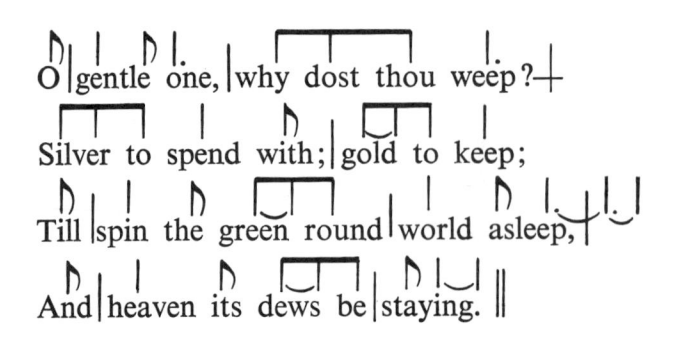

Finally, here is our tune. Notice that the first half ends on a note of the dominant chord. There is contrast in phrases three and four, reflecting the mood of the words, and a slight climax in the fifth phrase. The last phrase is a variant of the opening bars, giving balance and unity.

Moderato

As we dance round a-ring-a-ring, A maiden goes a-maying; And here a flower, and there a flower, Through mead and meadow straying: O gentle one, why dost thou weep? Silver to spend with; gold to keep; Till spin the green round world asleep, And heaven its dews be staying.

Set the following verses for your own voice, or the voices of some of your friends. Consider carefully the range and quality of the voice you are thinking of, and be sure to rehearse and perform your songs.

A New Year Carol

Here we bring new water
   from the well so clear,
For to worship God with,
   this happy New Year.
Sing levy dew, sing levy dew,
   the water and the wine;
The seven bright gold wires
   and the bugles that do shine.

Anon

Binnorie

There were two sisters sat in a bower,
   Binnorie, O Binnorie;
There came a knight to be their wooer,
   By the bonnie mill-dams of Binnorie.
He courted the eldest with glove and ring,
   Binnorie, O Binnorie;
But he loved the youngest above all thing,
   By the bonnie mill-dams of Binnorie.

Anon

The Schoolboy

I love to rise in a summer morn
   When the birds sing on every tree;
The distant huntsman winds his horn,
   And the skylark sings with me.
     O! what sweet company.

William Blake

When daffodils begin to peer,
   With heigh! the doxy over the dale,
Why then comes in the sweet o' the year;
   For the red blood reigns in the winter's pale.

'The Winter's Tale'

HARMONY

Sing this gay little song, and make up some verses of your own. (*OSMB Beginners*, Book III, page 14.)

Jovially

Roll that brown jug down to town, Roll that brown jug down to town,

Roll that brown jug down to town, So ear-ly in the morn-ing.

2 Ride that little bike down to town.   3. Walk that little dog home again.
4. Roll your little self down to school.

Which bars may be harmonized with the tonic chord?
Sing the notes of bars 3 and 4.

Notice that they form the notes of the dominant triad:

Root Third Fifth

Now consider bar 7:

The C is at an interval of a minor seventh from the root of the dominant chord:

minor 7th

Root 3rd 5th 7th

The chord now formed is the dominant seventh:

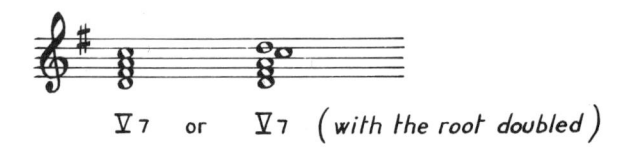

V7   or   V7 (*with the root doubled*)

The V7 sounds restless to move on to another chord, and because of this is called a DISCORD. When a discord is followed by another chord in a way that satisfies the listener, we say that the discord has been resolved, e.g.,

Notice particularly that the seventh falls a semitone, and the leading note rises a semitone.

Sing this as a round in your groups. Use the sol-fa syllables.

You are demonstrating the progression just discussed—V7 resolving on I—and you are singing it in two, then three, then four, and finally in five parts.

Now change the order of entries, e.g.

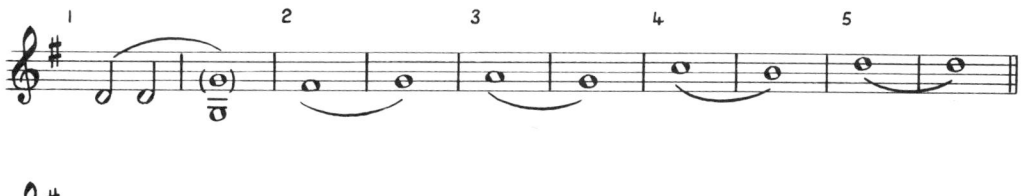

Begin the round again. Then let individuals sing the entries in any order they wish; they might stop singing for a few bars to listen to the progression and try to notice whether any of the five parts are missing.

It has been pointed out that in the progression V7–I, the seventh falls a semitone (*f* to *m*), and the leading note rises a semitone (*t* to *d*). It is also common practice for the dominant note to remain stationary, as in bars 1 and 2 of the first version of the round, unless it is in the bass, and for the supertonic to rise or fall one degree, as in bars 5 and 6.

With these points in mind, write, play, and sing resolutions to the following dominant sevenths:

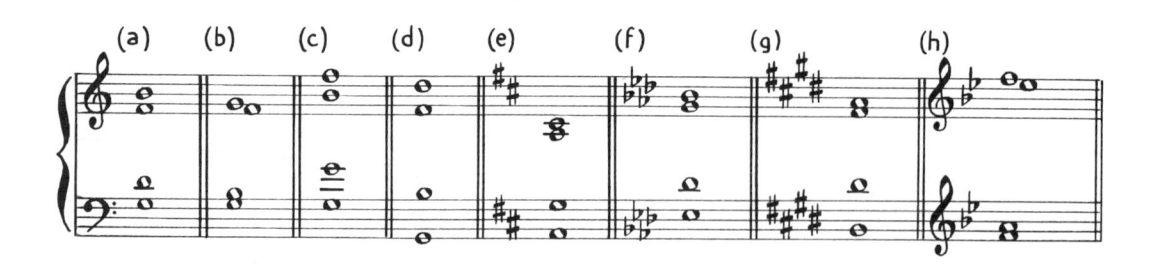

Here is part of a waltz by Schubert. It consists entirely of chords V7 and I in the keys of A flat and F:

Allegro moderato

Schubert, Walzer Op. 9

Let one of the group play the piano while the rest sing the following accompaniment, using sol-fa syllables.

Play the following three melodies in all the major keys, supplying chords V7 and I at the points indicated. Experiment with different spacings of your chords. Think pianistically, and at the same time remember to resolve the dominant sevenths correctly. Here are some suggestions for the first melody:

1. Moderato — Humperdinck, 'Hansel & Gretel'

V7 I

2. Con moto — The Sweet Nightingale

V7 I

3. Andante — Irish Melody

Oft in the stil-ly night, Ere slum-ber's chain has bound me

V — 7 I

Now let us return to our song, 'Roll that brown jug down to town', and provide it with a piano accompaniment.

We have examined its harmonic implications. Here it is then, showing the chords that we shall employ:

It is a jolly tune that moves at a lively pace. By ranging over the notes of our two triads in arpeggio-fashion, it has a 'rolling' gait which fits the words admirably. In these circumstances, perhaps the most suitable accompaniment will be one which avoids duplicating these features. Let us devise a simple harmonic background against which the tune can make its full effect.

Here is a simple three-part harmonization. It shadows the outline of the tune in bars 1 to 4 and becomes a little more independent in bars 5 to 8.

Taking this as our basis we can make it more pianistic by using more of the keyboard, by introducing more movement and rhythmic figuration, and by judicious use of the sustaining pedal. The following accompaniments illustrate these points. Notice that the notes are the same in each version, but the amount of movement varies, as do the pedalling, phrasing and dynamics. Practise them and memorize them. Then sing the song and accompany yourself.

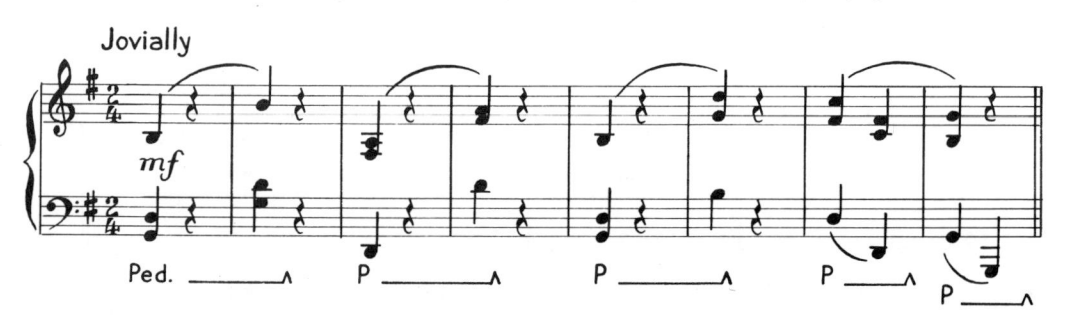

We may wish to have a thicker texture in our accompaniment for some verses. If so we can retain the outline of our three-part version, and increase its sonority by suitable doublings and different spacings in our chords:

Write and play accompaniments to these three songs:

1. Dramatically   English traditional song (OSMB Junior Bk. I)

There was an old man called Michael Finnigin; He grew whiskers on his chin-i-gin. The wind came up and blew them in-i-gin, Poor old Michael Fin-ni-gin, Be-gin-ni-gin, There

2. **In waltz time**
German folk-song
(OSMB Junior Bk. II)

O my little Au-gus-tin, Au-gus-tin, Au-gus-tin, O my little Au-gus-tin, ev'-ry-thing's gone! Our mo-ney and goods are gone, All we de-pend u-pon. O my little Au-gus-tin, ev'-ry-thing's gone.

3. **Leggiero**
German folk-song
(OSMB Junior Bk. II)

The birds all met to hold a wed-ding in a-mong the trees so green, fidi-ra-la-la, fidi-ra-la-la, fidi-ra-la-la-la-la.

We now return to the round that we sang earlier in this chapter, and, using the same harmonic framework, we begin to introduce more movement.

Sing the following in four parts:

Moderato

Notice:
   (1) the seventh is used as a passing note
   (2) the leading note goes to another factor of the chord before resolving on the tonic
   (3) the seventh goes to another factor of the chord before resolving on the third of I (i.e., the resolution is decorated)

using the same outline, we sing more passing notes:

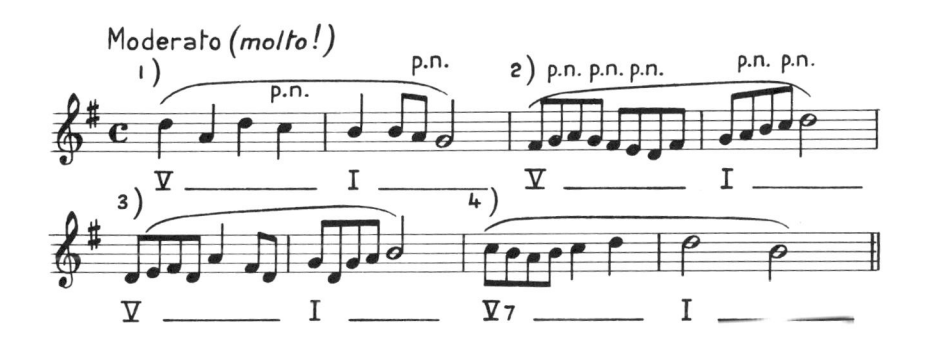

PASSING NOTES, as we explained in Chapter One, move by step from one note of a chord to another one third higher or one third lower. They are called UNESSENTIAL NOTES because they do not form a necessary factor in the basic structure of the harmony. They are decorative rather than functional (the icing on the cake).

In the first line of the above round, all the passing notes are indicated. The other notes belong to the harmonies indicated and are called HARMONY NOTES.

Say which of the notes in the second line are harmony notes, and which are passing notes.

Sing the round again, omitting all the passing notes. What is the difference in effect?

Another variety of unessential note that was introduced in Chapter One is the AUXILIARY NOTE.

Like a passing note, an auxiliary note moves by step away from the harmony note.

Unlike a passing note, the auxiliary note then *returns to the original harmony note*.

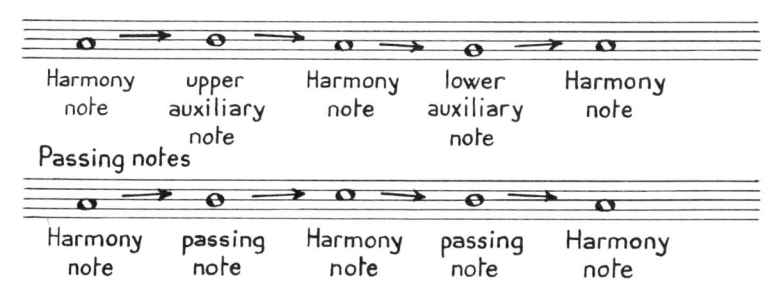

We now return to our round and incorporate auxiliary notes as well as passing notes:

[Musical notation: Moderato, with sections labeled 1), 2), 3), 4), marked with "a.n." annotations and V—I harmonic analysis]

Which are auxiliary and which passing notes in the second line?

With each of the following quotations:
(1) Decide on the key, and play I–V7–I, e.g.

[Musical notation: I–V7–I cadence in two staves]

(2) Sing the notes of the chords to sol-fa, e.g.

[Musical notation: Andante, with sol-fa syllables: d m s m d s₁ d   s₁ t₁ r f s   f r t₁   d s₁ d m d]

(3) Sing the melody:

Mozart, K.525

[Musical notation: Allegro, f]

(4) Let one student sing the melody whilst the others sustain the appropriate chords, e.g.

Let individual students write the chords to be sung on the blackboard, and conduct the singing.

1. Allegro — Quilter, Children's Overture

2. Andante — Schubert, Cradle Song

3. Moderato — Schubert, 'The Maid of the Mill'

4. Vivace — Mozart, Aria from 'Figaro'

5. Allegro — Weinberger, Fugue from 'Schwanda the Bagpiper'

Play the tonic chord and then try to hear each of the following tunes in your mind; then play the themes and harmonize with I and V7 chords. Which of the unessential notes are passing and which auxiliary?

38

1. Tempo di Gavotte — Bach, Suite N° 3 in G

2. Andante — Mozart, Don Giovanni

3. Allegro — Bach, Brandenburg Concerto N° 6 in B♭

4. Vivace — Weber, Invitation to the Dance

5. Molto allegro — Beethoven, Pianoforte Concerto N° 2 in B♭

Here are four bars of the string parts of the second movement of Haydn's 'Clock' Symphony, No. 101 in D. Continue the 'tick-tock' quavers in the uncompleted bars.

Here now is a more extended quotation for you to sing in your group:

Allegro — *sotto voce* — Mozart, 'Figaro'

Chorus: Come, all faith-ful lo-vers, and join us in song, To him who re-leas'd us from shame and from wrong. Our vir-tue pro-tect-ing, our hon-our re-spect-ing, That right he re-noun-ces which brought us dis-grace.

(V7b)

CHAPTER FOUR

MELODY

In the last chapter you were reminded of auxiliary notes and passing notes. Let us now go a stage further in our investigation of these two types of unessential notes. We will confine our examination to passages based on chords I, V, and V7.

Here are the first three bars of Mozart's overture to the opera *The Marriage of Figaro*.

This comic opera is full of movement, frivolous intrigue and misadventure. How skilfully Mozart conveys the essence of all this at the very outset! You will notice that the phrase is built around the D major triad. Themes based upon a major chord tend to convey feelings of pleasure and happiness and this phrase is no exception. But Mozart also wishes to convey a hint of other things; of mischief, secret assignations, startled retreats, and confusion. This he achieves by rapid pianissimo movement and a subtle use of crotchet rests. But any kind of rapid movement would not do. Imagine the effect of rapid leaps; these would hardly hint at sly conspiracy. Mozart requires smooth, flowing, step-wise movement and this can only be obtained by the use of auxiliary notes and passing notes. We need only study bar one to realize what character can be given to a single note when it is decorated with auxiliary notes, and fitted to an arresting rhythm.

Later in the overture at bar 133, Mozart has reached the end of his development section and is about to return to the opening theme quoted above. To prepare us for this return he stays on the chord of the dominant seventh for six bars. Here are the bare bones of the harmony:

Now see how interesting Mozart's version is. Notice that the quaver movement is produced by the use of passing and auxiliary notes.

Our next example comes from the last movement of Beethoven's Pastoral Symphony. The main theme of this rondo (A) appears later in the movement in an embroidered version (A¹). In both cases, the first three bars are based on the tonic chord and you will notice that in A¹, the beautiful flowing pastoral effect is obtained by decorating the triad with passing and auxiliary notes.

For our last example, let us turn to the opening of Bach's fourth Brandenburg Concerto. (We have extracted the parts for solo flutes and continuo from the full score.)

Here is a chordal progression based upon the harmonies used by Bach:

You will agree that this could hardly be duller. It is almost devoid of rhythm and melody. But if we substitute Bach's bass you will feel an immediate improvement and appreciate the craftsmanship which lies behind it. By ranging over two octaves, Bach produces a melody. Notice that the first phrase curves downwards to the low D in the sixth bar and this is balanced by a rising response. Notice too, that there are curves within these curves, but that each phrase has an over-all tendency to rise or fall. This makes it interesting to the performer and listener, since by its nature it asks to be moulded and phrased.

We now invent a melody with similar characteristics. We will aim at a flowing effect by limiting ourselves to step-wise movement together with the interval of a third. We will not forget to have a falling curve in the first phrase and to balance this by a rising one in the response.

Here is a second version. It has rather more energy because we have used the interval of a sixth. Again, notice the curve of each phrase.

With this harmonic progression firmly in our minds, let us proceed to write in two parts. We will invent a flowing melody. By using passing notes and auxiliary notes we can introduce step-wise quaver movement. We have to invent short rhythmic patterns. Suppose we search for two rhythmic ideas, each two bars long, which shall be contrasting yet complementary. We will embroider the outline of our previous melody based on sixths.

Let us now lighten the texture by introducing rests (remember that silences are often as important as sounds in music), and we will give the music more spring and buoyancy by changing the time-signature from $\frac{3}{4}$ to $\frac{3}{8}$.

We decided to invent rhythmic patterns of two bars in length. Suppose we now modify our melody and allow the first phrase to flow on for an extra bar, and then follow this by a two-bar phrase which grows out of the rhythm of the third bar. This reduces the squareness of our previous version. You should now begin to appreciate the artistry of Bach's rhythm in the Brandenburg Concerto.

Here are two basses that may be treated in the way we have just described. Write interesting, rhythmic melodies, supported by a continuo bass in the style of Bach. Use chords I, V, and V7, together with passing and auxiliary notes.

Compose melodies for the following verses. Write for your own voice or that of a friend. Rehearse and discuss your settings together: you may be able to improve your melodies after the experience of rehearsing them. Finally give a performance to your group.

Daybreak
Stay, O sweet, and do not rise!
  The light that shines comes from thine eyes;
The day breaks not: it is my heart,
  Because that you and I must part.
    Stay! or else my joys will die
    And perish in their infancy.
              John Donne (1573–1631)

Hey nonny no!

Hey nonny no!
Men are fools that wish to die!
Is't not fine to dance and sing
When the bell of death do ring?
Is't not fine to swim in wine,
And turn upon the toe,
And sing hey nonny no!
When the winds blow and the seas flow?
Hey nonny no!

      Christ Church MS

Madrigal

My love in her attire doth show her wit,
It doth so well become her;
For every season she hath dressings fit,
For Winter, Spring, and Summer.
 No beauty she doth miss
  When all her robes are on;
 But Beauty's self she is
  When all her robes are gone.

    Davison's 'Poetical Rhapsody' (1602)

The North Wind doth Blow

The north wind doth blow,
And we shall have snow,
And what will the robin do then, Poor thing?
 He'll sit in a barn,
 And keep himself warm,
And hide his head under his wing, Poor thing!

        Anon.

HARMONY

Add this folk-song to your repertoire. You will find that it is soon a favourite.

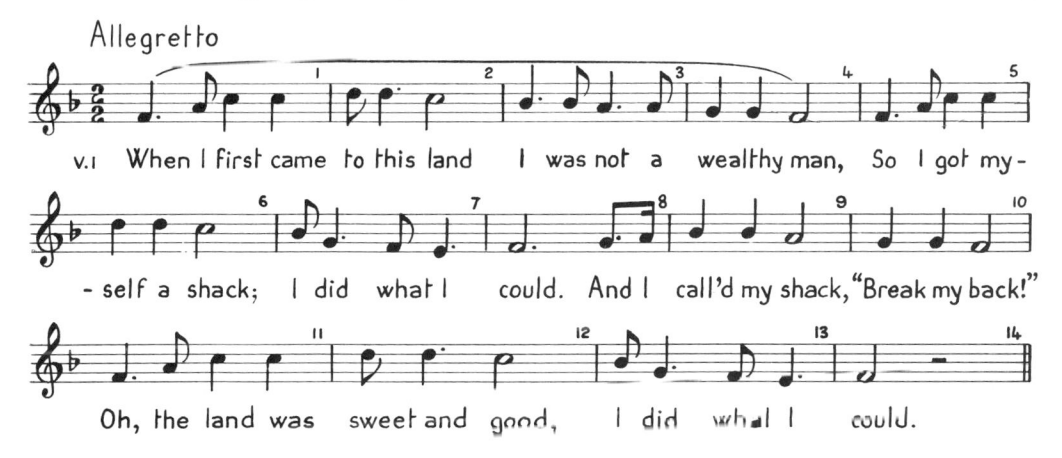

[Musical notation: Allegretto, bars 1–14]

v.1 When I first came to this land I was not a wealthy man, So I got my-self a shack; I did what I could. And I call'd my shack, "Break my back!" Oh, the land was sweet and good, I did what I could.

2. So I got myself a cow — And I called my cow 'No milk now!'
3. So I got myself a duck — And I called my duck 'Hard Luck!'
4. So I got myself a wife — And I called my wife 'Run for your life!'
5. So I got myself a son — And I called my son 'My work's done!'

Bars 9 and 10 are repeated once in the second verse, twice in the third, three times in the fourth, and so on, so that the 'And I called my —' lines from the previous verses may be sung again. To vary this part of the song, some members of the group might improvise other parts based on V–I or V7–I harmonies.

If we use the plain V chord, we have the choice of root position V, or first inversion Vb.

[Musical notation: V Vb]

V7, however, is available in four positions.
   Root position, V7; first inversion, V7b; second inversion, V7c; last inversion, V7d.

We must remember to arrange for the 'leaning' notes (the leading note and the seventh) to resolve appropriately.

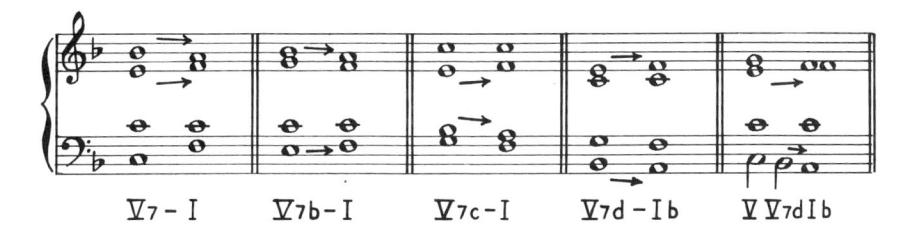

[Musical notation: V7–I, V7b–I, V7c–I, V7d–Ib, V V7dIb]

Try these arrangements:

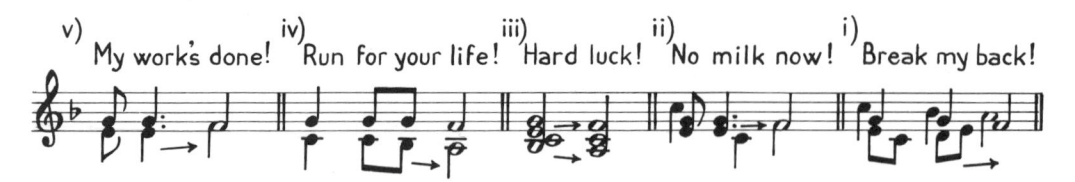

The following are the versions of V–I and V7–I that have been used above. Which ones apply to which verses?

    V7d–Ib;   Vb–V–I;   Vb(root absent)–I;

    Vb–V(p.n.)–V7b(root absent)–I;

    V(3rd absent)–V7d(root absent)–Ib.

(Answers at A on page 53)

Further variety may be obtained by harmonizing the G in bar 10 with two different harmonies. Here is a new chord to add to your vocabulary:

II7, like V7, is available in four positions. The seventh normally falls to the leading note.

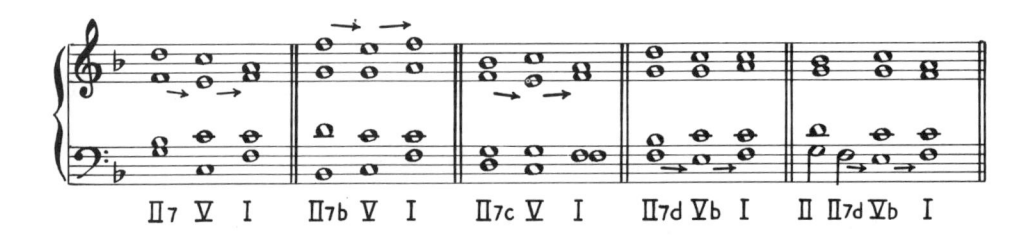

Sing these examples, first to sol-fa and then to the words above.

Here are the analyses of the examples just used. Which ones apply to which verses?

    117b–V, V7d(root absent)–Ib;   117c–V–Ib;   IIb–V(l.n. absent)–I;

    117b–V–Ib;   II, II7d–Vb, V(l.n. absent)–I.

(Answers at B on page 53)

Chord II is a minor chord ('minor' because the lowest interval is a minor third) and you will probably agree that it provides a pleasant change of flavour from the major chords that we have used so far.

Chord II is best used in its root position (II) or first inversion (IIb) and is most commonly followed by V or V7.

Sing, then play, and finally write down your analysis of these examples. (Answers at C.)

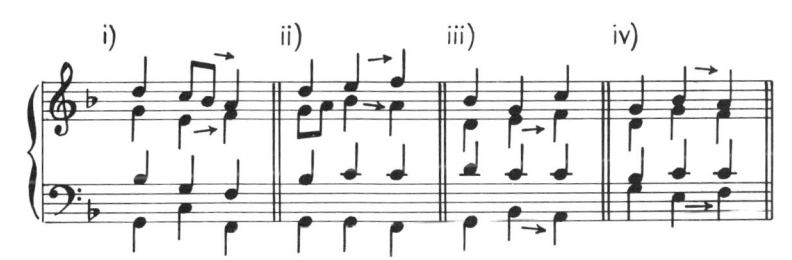

We continue to use arrows to show the leading note rising by step to the tonic and the seventh of the dominant seventh falling to the third of the tonic chord.

Chord II7 also leads effectively to V or V7 harmony. The seventh of the supertonic seventh, like the seventh of the dominant seventh, resolves by falling one step; the third, however, not being the leading note, need not rise.

The essential notes in II7 (as in V7), are the root and the seventh. II7 may be used in any position (II7, II7b, II7c, II7d).

Sing, play, and analyse these resolutions of the supertonic seventh. (Answers at D.)

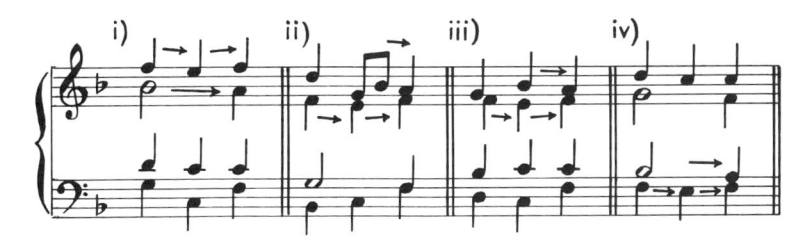

These examples are written in parts for four individual voices. The following are the ranges normally expected in a choir:

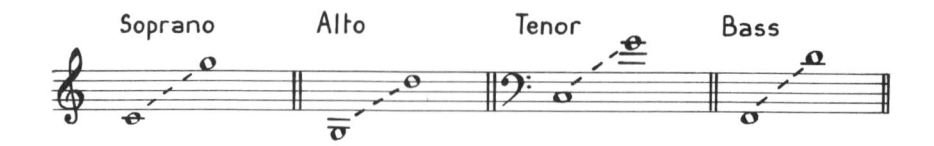

[Musical example showing Soprano, Alto, Tenor, Bass ranges]

If we are to keep each of the four parts independent, we shall avoid allowing any two parts to move in unison or octaves, e.g.

[Musical examples i), ii), iii), iv)]

In (i) the T and B are moving in unison ('consecutive unisons')
   (ii) the S and A are moving in unison ('consecutive unisons')
   (iii) the A and B are moving in octaves ('consecutive octaves')
   (iv) the S and T are moving in octaves ('consecutive octaves')
so that in these four examples there are only three real parts.

It was usual in classical music also to avoid writing movement in consecutive perfect fifths, though you will, of course, find plenty of examples of such progressions in medieval and modern music. The medieval musician, for example, preferred the sound of the fifth to that of the third, which he regarded as a dissonance. But in classical times consecutive perfect fifths were thought to be objectionable.

Since most systems of musical education take the classical idiom as the 'norm' in Western musical language, it is desirable that you should be able to write grammatically in this idiom, though this need not discourage you from also experimenting in other styles.

[Musical examples v), vi)]

In (v) the A and T are moving in consecutive perfect fifths
   (vi) the S and B are moving in consecutive perfect fifths

If you are to be quite sure that you have avoided consecutive unisons, octaves, and fifths, you must carefully check six pairs of parts. Which are they? (Answers at E.)

Harmonize for SATB and add appropriate indications of tempo and dynamics.

Now choose another key and write your own settings of all the progressions given in Answers Sections C and D. This work will prove most beneficial if groups arrange to sing, as vocal quartets, each student's solution while he listens to the effect.

Be sure that all the parts are within a reasonable compass for each voice and that all errors are eliminated before you show your work to your tutor.

Sing and study this example of five-part writing for voices.

---

* $\frac{5}{4}$ is usually felt to be $\frac{3}{4} + \frac{2}{4}$ or $\frac{2}{4} + \frac{3}{4}$ Be sure that you change harmonies on musically appropriate parts of the bar.

Sing we and chant it

Briskly
f (repeat *p*)

Thomas Morley

Sing we and chant it   While love doth grant it:

Fa la la la la la la la   Fa la la la.
Fa la la la la la la la la la la.
Fa la la la la la la la la.
Fa la la la la la la la la.
Fa la la la la la la la la la la.

Find examples of II and II7. (Answers at F.)

II7b in the penultimate bar progresses to V which in turn proceeds to I (V–I or V7–I is a 'musical full stop' or, more officially, a 'perfect cadence'). This is similar to the examples we have already practised.

II in bar I, however, is both preceded *and followed* by chord I (I–II–I). Play it slowly several times and savour the delicious effect.

The juxtaposition chords II and I often occurs in Elizabethan music and it is implied by the contours of many folk tunes. Consecutive perfect fifths and octaves are not objectionable in these styles, though in Elizabethan music they are usually decorated by such a device as 'the note of anticipation'.

Come again! Sweet love doth now invite

Brightly and rather fast — John Dowland

Come a-gain! Sweet love doth now in-vite.

Find the decorated consecutive perfect fifths in the above example.

SOLUTIONS

A. Verses (iii) (ii) (v) (i) (iv)
B. Verses (iv) (i) (v) (iii) (ii)
C. (1) II V I (2) II V7c I (3) II V7d Ib
   (4) II V7b I (5) IIb V7 I (6) IIb V7d Ib
   (7) IIb V7c I (8) IIb V7b I
D. (1) II7 V7 I (2) II7b V V7 I (3) II7c V7 I
   (4) II7d V7b I
E. S A; S T; S B; A T; A B; T B
F. Bar 1, beat 3—II
   Bar 7, beat 2—II7b

We must now begin to introduce chord II into our piano accompaniments. Here is a song from the Appalachian mountains.

The Deaf Woman's Courtship

Allegretto

Old wo-man, old wo-man, are you fond of smo-king?

Speak a lit-tle lou-der, sir, I'm ra-ther hard of hear-ing.

Sing it through, and then sing again to sol-fa syllables. Be able to play it fluently on the piano in a number of keys. As you play, try to feel the rhythm of the harmony—how often will the chords be sounded? Where will they change and where be repeated? Do you feel that the most suitable harmonic rhythm will be either

$$\frac{2}{4}\ \vert\ \partial\ \vert\ \partial\ \vert\ \partial\ \vert\ \partial\ \Vert$$

or

$$\frac{2}{4}\ \partial\ \vert\ \partial\ \vert\ \partial\partial\ \vert\ \partial\ \Vert$$

for each line?

You should feel that it would be most unmusical to have four different harmonies in the penultimate bar. Had you recognized the second quaver in this bar as an auxiliary note?

Bars 1, 2, and 4 of each line obviously call for the tonic chord, but in bar 3 of each line we have a choice of chord. We may use II or V or both these chords, and II may have its seventh if we wish (the dominant seventh is, of course, present in the tune).

Here then are some of the combinations of II and V from which we may choose. Try them all at the piano and see which you prefer. Follow this piano style as you experiment:

```
      V   – V7
      Vb  – V7
      II  –
      II  – V7
      IIb – V7
      II7b– V7
      II7c– V7
      II7d– V7b
```

In making your choice you have to consider what is appropriate for this simple little folk-song. II7d, for example, is a beautiful chord, and a strong chord. It can be most powerful in a stately chorale; you might think it out of place here. Harmony is often not a question of right and wrong, but one of fitness.

There is one point, however, on which we should agree; namely, that no matter what chords we decide upon, we should not make bar 7 a repetition of bar 3. In all your music-making you should cultivate a feeling for rise and fall, tension and relaxation. We saw earlier in the chapter how Bach put shape and feeling into a bass part built out of two notes. In our folk song we can achieve a sense of climax by aiming towards bar 7. In other words, if we use a simple chord in bar 3, and a more colourful one in bar 7, we shall have introduced a simple form of harmonic tension. The melody is repetitive but the harmony supplies the climax.

Keeping this in mind we will therefore base our accompaniment upon the following progression:

I–I–Vb, V7–I   I–Ib–II7b, V7–I

In order to distinguish between the two characters in the song we will get a contrast of texture, tempo and intensity between the question and answer:

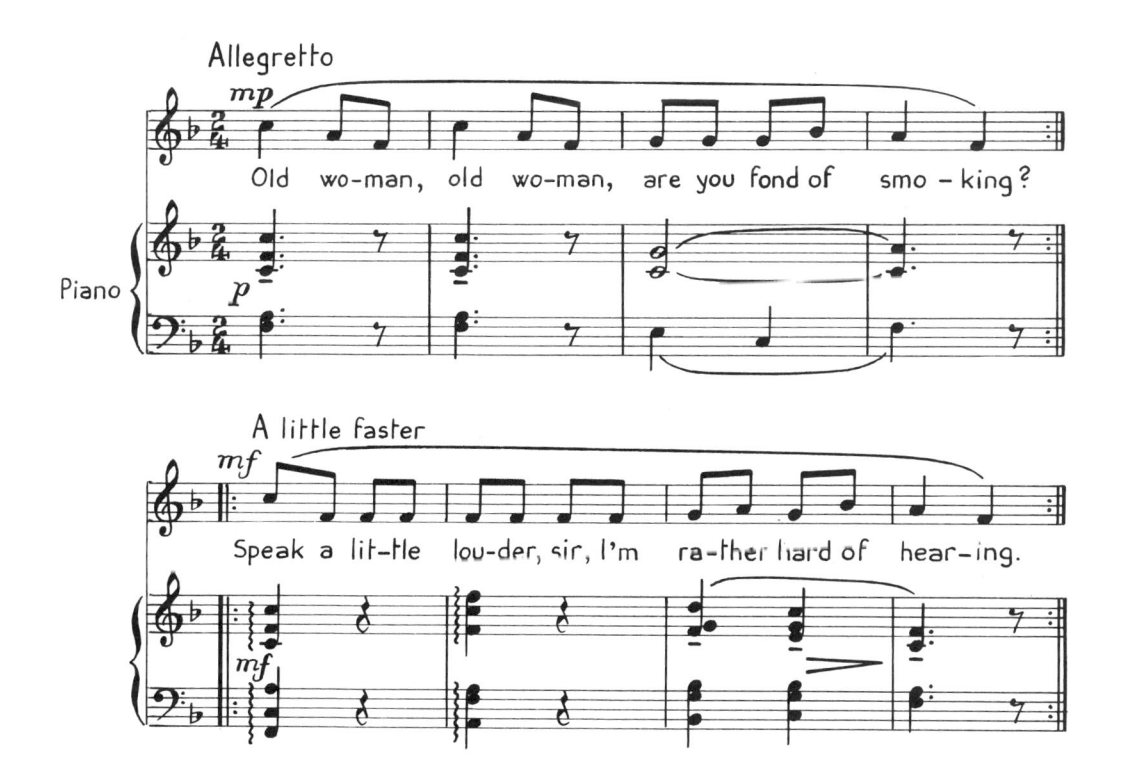

Practise singing the song to your own accompaniment. Here are some songs for further practice. Write out your accompaniments and see that they are carefully phrased and edited.

1. Allegretto — OSMB Junior Bk. I

Tra-ra, the Post has come! Tra-ra, the Post has come! From far I hear him blow his horn, From far its gal-lant sound is born, He blows it lou-der still; He blows it with a will, The Post has come, tra-ra, tra-ra, The Post has come, tra-ra!

2. Andante — OSMB Junior Bk. I

Go and tell Aunt Nan-cy, Go and tell Aunt Nan-cy, Go and tell Aunt Nan-cy, The old grey goose is dead.

More tunes to sing and harmonize:

3. Allegretto — 'Under the Spreading Chestnut Tree' English Trad.
(used by Weinberger in 'Variations and Fugue on an Old English Tune')

4. Allegro molto — Schubert, Symphony No 5 in B♭

5. Giocoso — Humperdinck, 'Hansel and Gretel'

Bro-ther, come and dance with me, Both my hands I of-fer thee, Right foot first, Left foot then, Round a-bout and back a-gain.

6. Allegro   Mozart, Aria from 'Figaro'

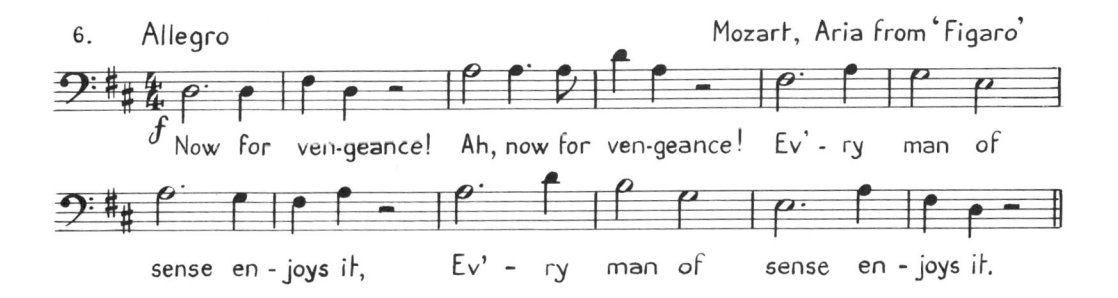

f Now for ven-geance! Ah, now for ven-geance! Ev'-ry man of sense en-joys it, Ev'-ry man of sense en-joys it.

Fiddle Tunes

Ask a violinist to play the tunes that follow while you improvise rhythmic accompaniments. Alternatively, ask a pianist to play the tunes an octave higher, or on a second pianoforte.

Listen to recordings of The Country Dance Band in the H.M.V. Folk Dance Series, and try to catch the style of playing. Join in with the records by quietly playing the melody or harmony.

Play other tunes from the *Fiddler's Tune Books* and from *Community Dance Manuals* I–VI (English Folk Dance and Song Society). Read the introductions to these books.

The Steamboat

The De'il among the Tailors
(B music)

The Irish Washerwoman

In the quotations that follow, play the tonic chord and then try to hear each theme in your mind; then play the theme and harmonize it with I, II(7), and V(7).

Quotations from orchestral compositions

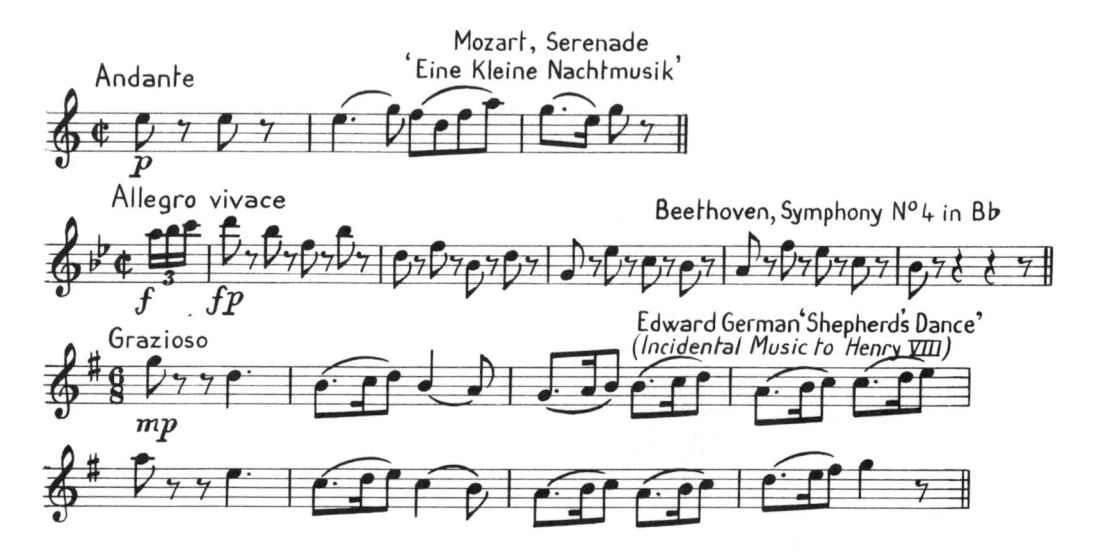

Quotations from pianoforte sonatas

Sumer is icumen in

Rehearse and study this remarkable composition. Relish again the I–II–I progression already met in quotations from folk and Elizabethan music. Read the following note by W. G. Whittaker:

' "Summer is icumen in" occurs in a Reading Abbey manuscript, the date of which is considered to be 1240, although some experts place it ten or more years earlier. It is in six parts, the four upper ones being a canon or round, and the two lower a ground-bass, also in canon, with an independent theme. Grove's Dictionary remarks: "In six directions is it pre-eminent, for (i) it is the oldest known canon; (ii) it is the oldest known harmonized music which is frequently performed and enjoyed by singers and listeners to-day; (iii) it is the oldest known six-part composition; (iv) it is one of the oldest known specimens of the use of what is now the major mode; (v) it is the oldest known specimen of ground bass; (vi) it is the oldest known manuscript in which both secular and sacred words are written to the music". The original words (which have been slightly altered in this edition) were in Wessex dialect, and a Latin text was adopted, "presumably to make this musical gem available for performance within the Abbey Church". The ground is reproduced here in the left-hand piano part. The top line should be learned first in unison, and when it is mastered the class divided into four parts. As soon as the vocal parts are secure, the accompanist should only play the left-hand part, with the E♭.F.E♭ always doubled at the 8ve below. Two male voices can replace this by singing throughout the following in canon:

Sing cuck - oo, now sing cuck - oo.

one voice beginning at the first bar and the other simultaneously at the fifth. An effective way of singing the present version is for the choir to sing the top line right through first, in unison, unaccompanied, and then as printed.'

Swingingly, one slow beat in a bar
I
II
VOICES
III
IV
p
Sum-mer is a - com-ing in, — Loud-e sing cuck-oo,
p
Sum-mer is a - com-ing in, —
Allegretto
PIANO
p

Grow-eth seed and blow-eth mead, And spring the woodes new;
Loud-e sing cuck - oo, Grow-eth seed and blow-eth mead, And
p
Sum-mer is a - com-ing in, — Loud - e sing cuck - oo,
p
Sum-mer is a - com-ing in, —

61

f
Mer-ry sing cuck-oo; Cuck - oo, Cuck - oo,
dim.
Bul-lock start-eth, buck-e ver - teth, Mer-ry sing cuck-oo.
af - ter calf - e cow; Bul-lock start-eth, buck-e ver-teth,
Ewe-e bleat-eth af - ter lamb, Loweth af-ter calf - e cow.
mf dim.
Well sing - es thou cuck - oo, Nor cease thou ne - ver now.
Cuck - oo, Cuck - oo, Well sing thou cuck - oo.
Mer - ry sing cuck-oo; Sing cuck - oo.
Bul - lock start-eth, buck - e ver- teth, Mer - ry sing cuck - oo.
pp

CHAPTER FIVE

HARMONY

We now return to the folk-song 'When I first came to this land', which we met in the last chapter, and consider the harmonization of the first line.

The supertonic triad sounds out of place in this context.

The following is preferable. Memorize this harmonization and play it in other keys:

The new chord that we have introduced is the SUBDOMINANT (like the tonic and dominant, a major triad), and our harmonic vocabulary now consists of:

*These three major triads are known as the PRIMARY TRIADS.

Sing the first line of the folk-song and accompany yourself, first in the key of F, and then in F sharp, G, E, and E flat.

Vary the accompaniment by introducing rests, using a wider range of pitch, making use of legato and staccato styles, etc.

Sing the following fragments to the sol-fa syllables, and then harmonize them at the piano. If you recognize the quotation, complete it yourself. Otherwise, improvise an answering phrase. We show some of the alternative harmonies possible. Try them all and decide which you prefer. Experiment with other notes too.

1. Lightly — Paul's Little Hen (Danish)

2. Quickly

3. In a strong rhythm

4. Allegretto
Appalachian
l r d l,
Ib IV Ib I Ib V7b I IV
V7d Ib
IIb Ib

5. Andante
Scottish
r m l,
IV I
IV V7d

6. Allegro
Appalachian
l,
IV I
IV V
IV II V
II(7) II7 V

7. Allegro
Scottish
l
IV Ib V7c I II V
IV V V7d Ib I IV V

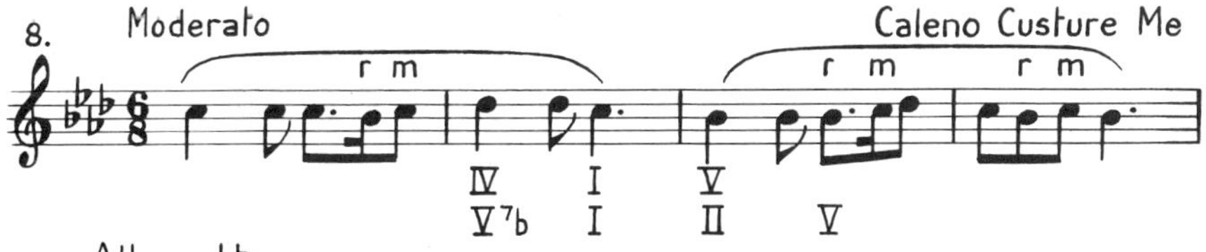
8. Moderato
Caleno Custure Me
r m r m r m
IV I V
V7b I II V

9. Allegretto
English Folk Carol
l
II7b V
IV I

10. Andante
The Ash Grove
l

11. Andante
Scottish
l

12. Andante
The London Watchman's Song
l r m

13.

14.

15.

When the progression IV–I comes at the end of a phrase, we have a PLAGAL CADENCE. This is the cadence often used for 'Amen' after a hymn.

In Nos. 5, 6, and 9 above, we have indicated choices between plagal and imperfect cadences. In each case say which you consider to be the more appropriate.

In No. 8 there is a choice between a perfect and a plagal cadence. Which do you prefer?

Complete for four voices and then compare your version with that of the composer:

(i) The plagal cadence

16.

17.

(ii) Progressions including chords I, II, IV, and V

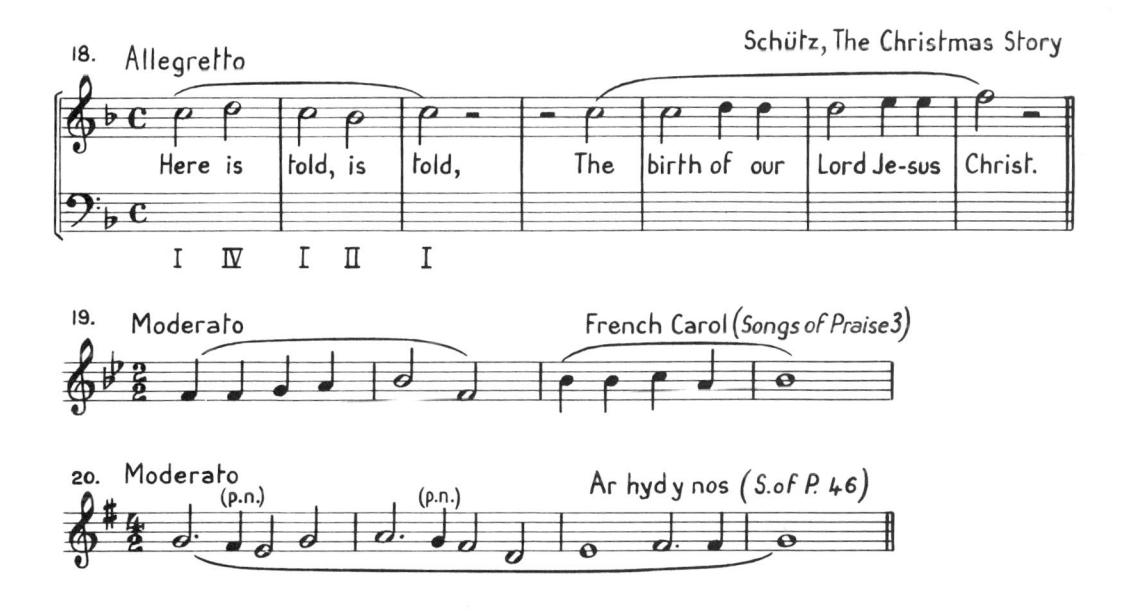

18. Allegretto — Schütz, The Christmas Story

Here is | told, is | told, | — | The | birth of our | Lord Je-sus | Christ.

I IV I II I

19. Moderato — French Carol (Songs of Praise 3)

20. Moderato (p.n.) (p.n.) — Ar hyd y nos (S. of P. 46)

MELODY

The Submediant—*Lah*

Lah plays an important role in the gay, dance-like tunes numbered 1, 2, and 9, in the festive and exalted hymn tunes, Nos. 14 and 15, and in the climax of No. 11 (c.f. the last phrase of the National Anthem).

Lah, is pensive in Nos. 5 and 12, and sturdy in No. 6.

Lah and *lah*, are beautifully contrasted in No. 4.

The Supertonic—*Ray*

Ray is restless to move on to another note. Sing some of the above tunes again, and this time pause on *ray*; feel the urge to move on.

In Nos. 3, 4, and 15, *ray* proceeds directly to *doh*. More interesting is the progression of *ray* to *me*, as in Nos. 5, 8, and 12, and at the end of the first phrase in No. 14.

Ray is frequently harmonized with chord II or chord V, and other factors of these chords are often heard between *ray* and its resolution on to *doh* or *me*. Study the progression of *ray* in Nos. 1 and 10 and say which harmonies are implied.

The Pentatonic Scale

Many of the world's finest folk melodies are based upon a five-note scale, *d r m s l*, called the pentatonic scale. This grouping is easily found if one plays the black notes of the pianoforte, beginning on F sharp:

Note the gaps—minor thirds—and that the step-movement is always in major seconds. There are no semitones.

Find the same patterns beginning on other notes, e.g.,

This scale makes an attractive fragment of melody in itself. However the order of the notes is changed, the result is invariably mellifluous.

Perhaps you already have this famous tune in your repertoire! Use only the second finger of each hand:

This beautiful Irish folk-song is also pentatonic:

The pentatonic scale is gentle and soothing, lacking the conflicts and tensions needed in a dramatic or developed style.

The following spirituals, quoted by Michael Tippett in his oratorio *A Child of Our Time* (Schott), are pentatonic. Tippett's harmonization, however, includes all the notes of the major scale. Note particularly the telling effect of the leading note in the alto, bass, and solo soprano parts.

Refer back to the twenty quotations included earlier in this chapter. Which of them are pentatonic? You should find six. Check that you are right by playing them on the black keys.

Primitive and oriental melodies

Sing these pentatonic melodies. Decide upon the dynamics and phrasing that you think appropriate. Let each student prepare and rehearse one of these melodies.

For further study of ancient and oriental music, consult the *New Oxford History of Music*, Volume I and the *History of Music in Sound* (H.M.V.), Volume I.

Tunes to sing and harmonize

Which of these tunes are not pentatonic?

Pentatonic melodies from romantic and modern music

Allegro ma non troppo — Dvořák, Quartet in F

Vivace — Chopin, Etude Op. 10, N° 5

Largo — Dvořák, Symphony in E min. (From the New World)

Cadenza for solo violin — Vaughan Williams, The Lark Ascending

In 'Laideronnette, Impératrice des Pagodes', the third movement of *Ma mère l'Oye*, Ravel makes extensive use of the pentatonic scale. This movement will repay careful study.

Here are the main themes:

Mouv.^t de Marche ♩ = 116
Piccolo solo (sounding an 8^{ve} higher)

The *Mother Goose* suite was first written as a piano duet in 1908, and was later scored for orchestra by Ravel. One would never guess that the second version was a transcription, so masterly is Ravel's skill as an orchestrator.

Notice the meticulous attention to phrasing. Ravel obviously understands the instruments for which he writes, and allots them melodies suited to their capabilities and expressive qualities.

Let us examine each of our four quotations with this in mind. The piccolo evokes the Oriental atmosphere of the movement. It has a rather mechanical, 'chopsticks', kind of tune. Notice that it is asked to play softly; the higher, shrill notes of the instrument are not involved; there are no nuances. The result is typically Eastern.

The oboe does not have an extended tune to play, but what it has is very much in character. The phrases are short and pithy. Staccato notes are prominent, with occasional telling accents. The melody lies within an effective part of the oboe's compass. There is a hint of humour.

The flute has a glorious tune; this must be one of the finest pentatonic tunes in instrumental music. Notice how it soars and curves over two-and-a-half octaves. Notice, too, the long, flowing, legato phrases with their crescendos and diminuendos. The flute plays in both its high and low registers. The lowest notes of the flute are rich and expressive. Try to hear a performance of this melody.

The clarinet, too, has an expressive, cantabile melody. It lies within the bottom register of the clarinet (the 'chalumeau' register) where the tone is particularly rich and arresting in quality.

Find out as much as you can about the characteristics of woodwind instruments. Consult such standard works as:

Orchestral Technique	Gordon Jacob
Orchestration	Cecil Forsyth
Orchestration	Walter Piston
Woodwind Instruments and their History	Anthony Baines

Begin to compose melodies for different woodwind instruments. Here are some suggestions for pentatonic melodies:

CHAPTER SIX

HARMONY

Here is a familiar progression; you will remember that we used it in the accompaniment to 'The Old Woman's Courtship' (Chapter Four).

Here is the same progression as used by Brahms in one of his 'Liebeslieder-Walzer', Op. 52.

You will notice that on the first beats of bars two, three and four, the singers have notes which do not belong to the basic harmony. These notes are APPOGGIATURAS, or 'leaning' notes.

The appoggiatura is one of the most expressive and important ornaments in music and its chief characteristics should be well understood.

(1) It is a dissonance, and is sounded on a strong beat.
(2) It demands a resolution, and 'leans' towards the harmony note that it has delayed. The resolution occurs on a weaker beat than that on which the appoggiatura was sounded.
(3) Some appoggiaturas lean towards a note a tone or semitone below; others reach upwards to a note a semitone above.

These points are well illustrated in the Brahms waltz. Notice particularly the expressive effect of the appoggiaturas. By their means Brahms not only suggests the lilt of the Viennese waltz, but also conveys the yearning of the lover. ('As the sunset burns in splendour so my heart would burn for thee")

Appoggiaturas are often printed in small type. The very appearance of the printed page enables us to distinguish clearly between the ornament and the harmony note it embellishes.

[Musical example: Menuetto — Mozart, K.282]

This type of notation reminds us that in earlier times performers were free to exercise their discretion in the execution of ornaments. Since the time of Haydn, the element of improvisation in musical performance has declined. Composers have gradually abandoned musical 'shorthand', and most ornaments are now noted down exactly as they are meant to be performed. Notation no longer draws attention to the presence of an appoggiatura; it is something we have to feel for ourselves.

Here, for example, is a well-known song in its usual notation:

[Musical example: Moderato — "Blow, blow thou win-ter wind."]

This is how it might have been noted down in an earlier century:

[Musical example: Moderato]

In this version it is plain to see which are the notes to be harmonized, and you can appreciate how important it is to be able to distinguish intuitively between an appoggiatura and the harmony note that it leans upon.

Here then is the outline of our melody together with some simple supporting harmonies:

[Musical example: Moderato — Vb I IV V]

If we now reintroduce the appoggiaturas we get:

Notice particularly the final chord in this phrase. It is the chord we would normally expect at the end of an opening phrase, namely V. Here it is decorated with an appoggiatura. Suppose we add a second appoggiatura, so that our inside part moves in parallel sixths with the melody:

The chord we have now produced on the first beat of the last bar is a second inversion chord. We made a brief reference to it in Chapter Two. Here are the three positions of the triad of F major:

The chord in the Arne melody is, therefore, the chord of Ic; and here we see it in its most important role, namely, as an appoggiatura chord, where the sixth leans down a tone, and the fourth leans down a semitone while the bass note remains stationary. The chord of V has been ornamented with a double appoggiatura.

Notice too, that the appoggiatura chord comes at the end of the phrase, i.e., at the cadence. This type of $^6_4$ is known as a 'cadential' $^6_4$ and is found in both imperfect and perfect cadences.

Here are various arrangements of these cadences. Play them in a number of keys and memorize them. You should be really familiar with these orthodox resolutions before we go on to discuss less usual procedures.

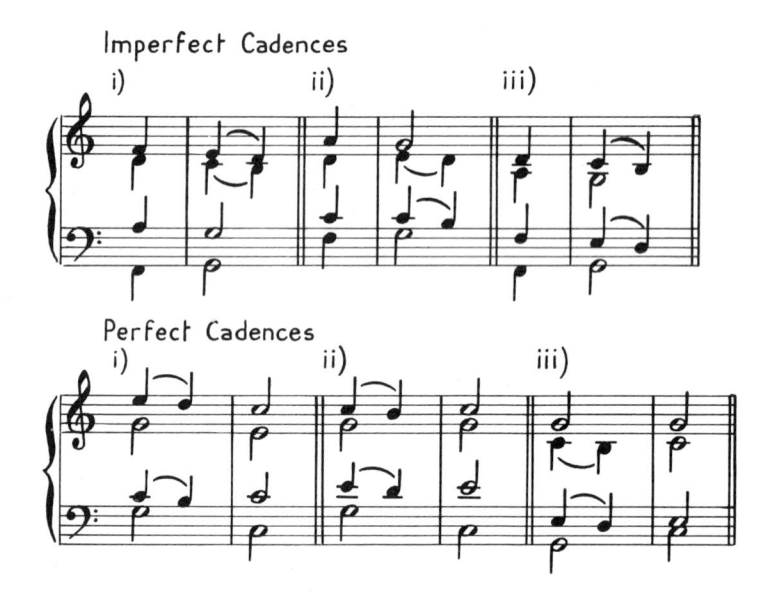

Play the following phrases, and end each one with a cadential $^6_4$. Transpose them into various keys.

8. Allegro — Humperdinck

9. Adagio — Mozart, K.576

10. Moderato — Mozart, 'Figaro'

You will find it instructive to study the scores of the great masters and note how they treat the cadential $^6_4$. Begin by perusing the first movement of Mozart's pianoforte sonata in C, K. 330.

You will find that the great composers do not always resolve Ic in the ways we have described. One particular variant is often used and provides the clue to most of the others. Here it is in its basic form:

Ic V^7

Most irregular resolutions of Ic arise from the presence of the dominant seventh. On these occasions, the part that has the sixth in Ic usually rises a semitone to the dominant seventh. Very often, as in our example, the fourth in Ic rises also to the fifth in chord V.

Moderato e grazioso — Beethoven, Rondo Op.51, Nº1

Allegro vivace — Schubert, Sonata Op.164

Finally, here are three elaborated versions of the cadential $^6_4$ for your consideration:

a) Andante — Mozart, K.533

b) Allegro — Mozart, K.333

c) Adagio — Mozart, K.576

Exercises

Harmonize these tunes at the keyboard, introducing a cadential $^6_4$ where appropriate.

1. Allegretto — German Folk Song

2. Allegro — Begone, dull care

3. Moderato

Here are two passages for you to sing. Notice that in each we find two balancing phrases—a statement ending with an imperfect cadence, and a response ending with a perfect cadence—and that a cadential $^6_4$ is employed at the end of each phrase.

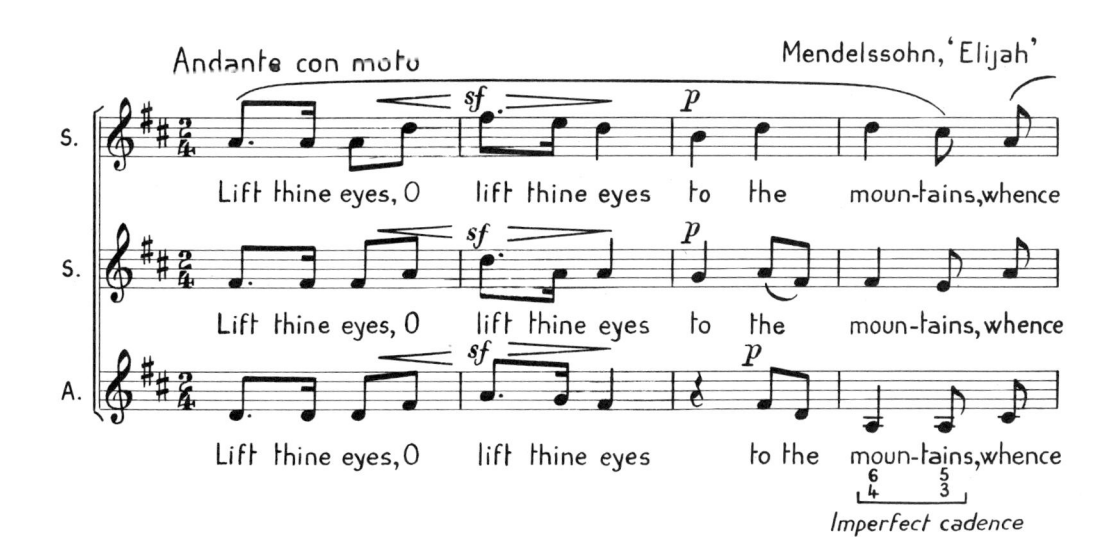

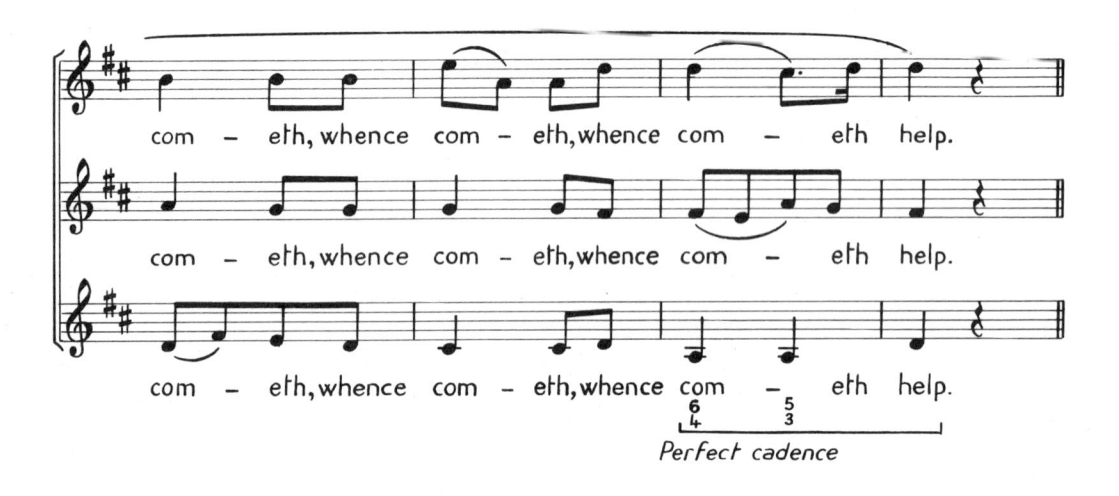

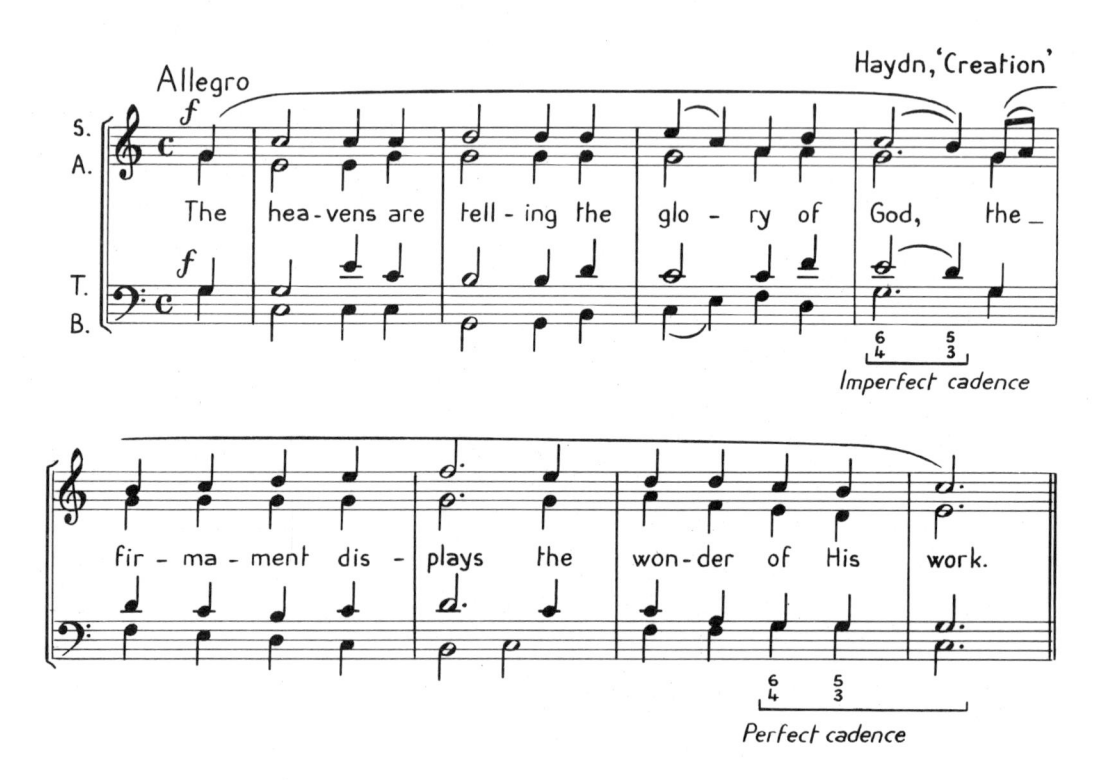

Here is the whole of the Brahms waltz that you met at the beginning of the chapter. Rehearse and perform it.

83

Thou, oh thou ___ a - lone canst ren - der

(Thou, oh thou)

All the joy ___ of life ___ for me. me.

Notice particularly the expressive effect produced by the leaning notes in bars 2, 3, 4, 6, 7, 14, and 15.

Notice too:

(a) The graceful, flowing quaver movement in the accompaniment. Since most of the quavers are harmony notes, the piano's embroideries are unobtrusive and do not detract from the charm and simplicity of the voice parts.

(b) The harmonic rhythm. There is one chord per bar for most of the time, but in bars 6, 7, and 15 we find two harmonies per bar. This slight variation in the rate of harmonic change is sufficient to prevent monotony without destroying the unity of the piece.

(c) The rhythm of the bass part in Piano II. The amount of movement is reduced in bars 9–12. This slackening of tension gives repose and at the same time prepares for the climax in the final phrase. Similarly, there are no appoggiaturas in bars 9–12, thereby adding to their effectiveness when they return towards the end.

Compose a Viennese waltz for piano. Experiment in the use of appoggiaturas. Do not always use them singly. Try the effect of double appoggiaturas in parallel thirds and sixths.

Add alto, tenor, and bass to these hymn tunes. Use the cadential $^6_4$ where appropriate.

1. Dignified — S. Webbe, Tantum Ergo (S.P., 199)

2. Moderately slow — J. D. Edwards, Rhosymedre (S.P., 127)

3\. In moderate time — C. Kocher, Dix (S.P. 83)

4\. Moderately slow — Praxis Pietatis Melica (S.P. 38)

5\. Rhosymedre (S.P. 127)

6\. New Sabbath (S.P. 691)

7\. Helmsley (S.P. 65)

CHAPTER SEVEN

HARMONY

The three minor triads on II, III, and VI of the major scale are known as SECONDARY TRIADS, as distinct from the three major PRIMARY TRIADS on IV, V, and I.

The word 'secondary' is largely a matter of terminology; it is not an aesthetic judgement. Do not be misled by the word into thinking that minor triads are in some way less satisfactory than major ones; that they are only to be used, 'faute de mieux', when primary triads prove unavailing.

Be positive in your approach to secondary triads. Use them freely. Enjoy them for their individual qualities, and for the colour and variety they can bring to your music. Remember that major and minor are complementary features of music, and are equally important. Only when both are present can music express the full range of human emotions.

Consider the following passages:

In (a) the bass part rises a tone from IV to V and falls a fifth from V to I. This pattern is reproduced in (b) as the bass moves II– III– VI. In (a) we have a familiar form of the perfect cadence, and, similarly, because of the way in which the bass moves, (b), too, has a cadential quality. Remember then, that III and VI and II and VI go well together, as do most progressions whose roots are a fourth or a fifth apart. This is demonstrated in the following examples:

Can you hear a woodwind instrument playing this tune?

We have chosen these particular quotations because minor chords are such a prominent feature of Russian folk music. When nineteenth-century Russian composers decided to form a national school, they took folk music as a basis for their compositions. If you wish to deepen your appreciation of minor harmonies you should certainly make yourself familiar with music from this Russian school.

Many of their melodies are modal and show the influence of early church music. We shall discuss this in a later chapter. In the meantime we confine ourselves to the use of secondary triads in the harmonization of diatonic melodies in the major key.

Secondary triads are particularly useful:

(a) in harmonizing repeated phrases,

[Musical example: a) Moderato — "The Fox and the Grapes", with chord analysis IV—I, IV—I]

[Musical example: b) with chord analysis VI—III, II—VI]

(b) in harmonizing a long or repeated *d* or *s*,

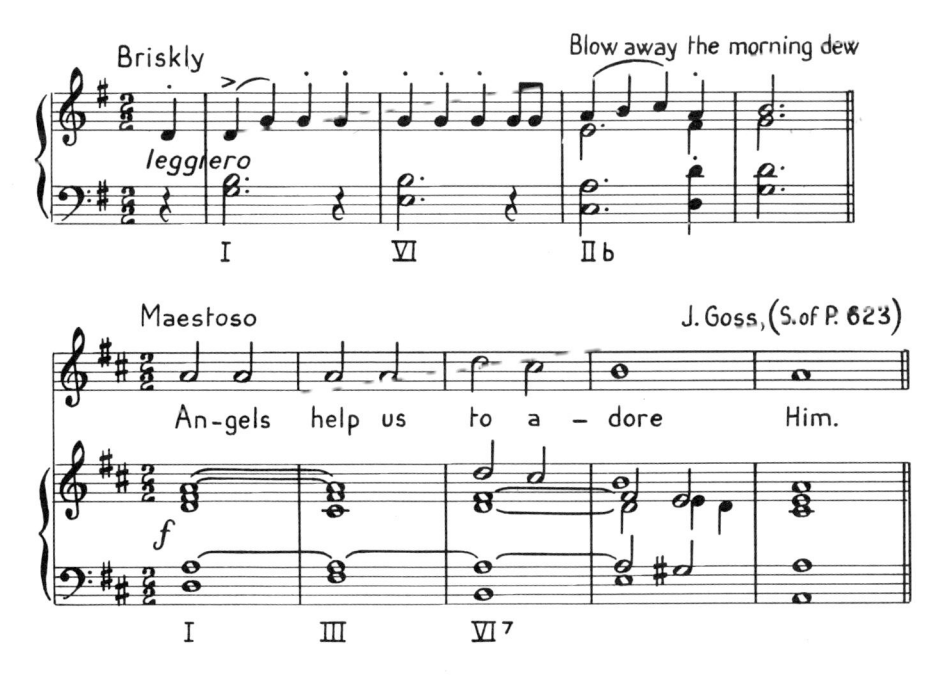

[Musical example: Briskly, leggiero — "Blow away the morning dew", with chord analysis I, VI, IIb]

[Musical example: Maestoso — "An-gels help us to a-dore Him." J. Goss, (S. of P. 623), with chord analysis I, III, VI⁷]

(The last two bars cannot be explained in terms of the progressions we have so far studied, but perhaps you can say what has happened.)

(c) in harmonizing the descending scale,

i)

I   III   IV   Ib   II⁷   Ic   V⁷   I

*The seventh remains in the following chord.

ii)

I   III   VI   Ib   IV   IIIb   V   I

Compare (i) and (ii). Which of the chord progressions do you prefer? Why? Sing the bass lines. Which do you prefer? Why?

(d) in a climax, especially when a pause or an allargando might be appropriate,

Blow away the morning dew

III   VI

(e) when an unexpected or inconclusive effect is needed,

i)   ii)

V — VI   V   I

Example (i) shows the INTERRUPTED, or SURPRISE CADENCE, sometimes called the FALSE CLOSE.

Example (ii) shows the conclusive PERFECT CADENCE.

The submediant chord comes as a surprise after the dominant chord because the ear is expecting, (a) a major chord and (b) the familiar s–d progression in the bass. Instead it hears a minor chord and the striking s–l.

The progression III–VI gives an effective alternative to the interrupted cadence V–VI.

Note that it is effective to double the minor third in chord VI in the interrupted cadence.

(f) to induce a solemn, majestic, or otherwise impressive style,

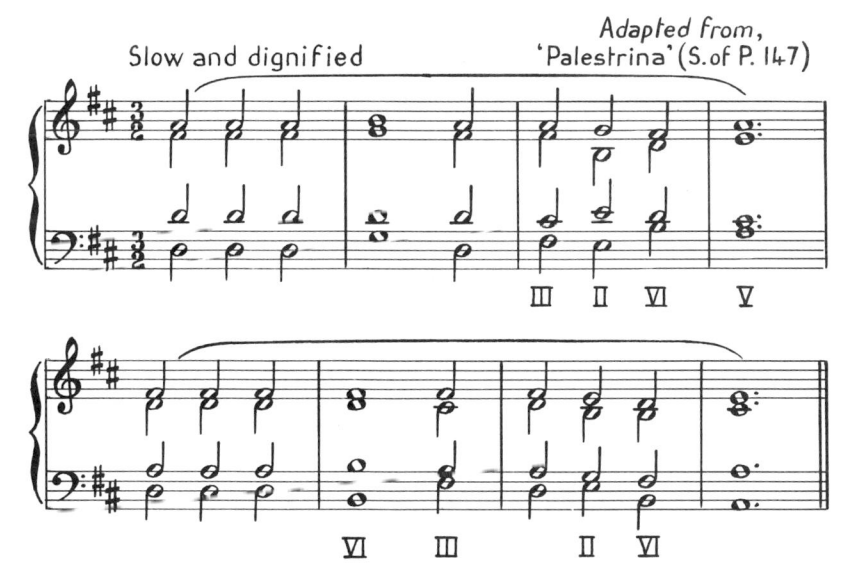

What do you notice **about the tenor melody** in the second line?

(g) in harmonizing melodies with m–d in a perfect or interrupted cadence.

The passing note introduced in (ii) causes these notes to be sounding together:

This chord sounds more like a strong version of V7 than the rather pale IIIb. It is, in fact, the DOMINANT THIRTEENTH (V13).

If we play all the notes of V13 together, we have a dissonant chord which contains every note of the scale

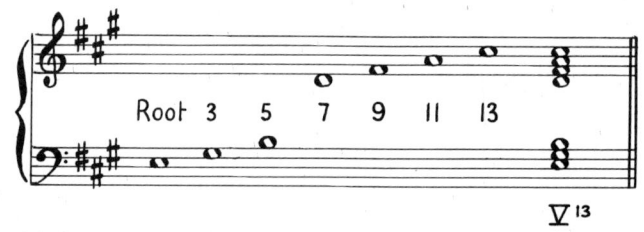

Let us decide which notes to keep, and which to dispense with.

Obviously we must keep the root and the thirteenth. The seventh gives the characteristic V7 flavour:

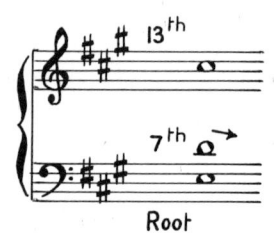

The third and eleventh conflict violently. Which is more appropriate in dominant harmony, the leading note or the tonic?

We decide to keep the leading note:

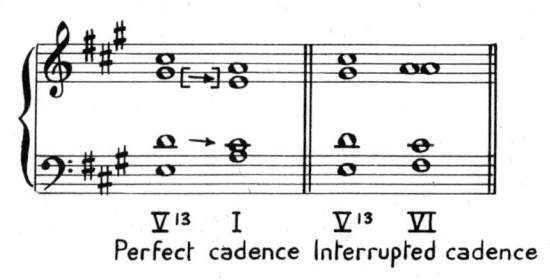

V13　I　　V13　VI
Perfect cadence　Interrupted cadence

We now consider the fifth and the ninth:

The fifth seems to provide only confusion and congestion. The thirteenth is best used instead of, rather than as well as, the fifth.

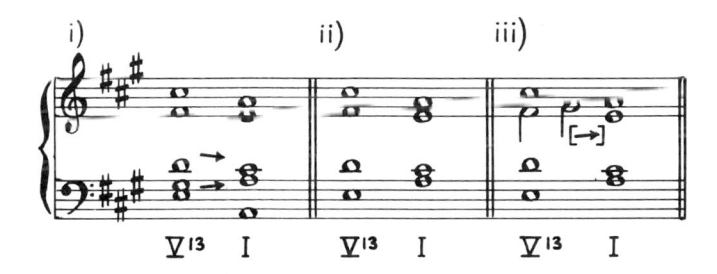

The ninth is effective either (i) in five-part writing in addition to the leading note, (ii) instead of the leading note, or (iii) progressing to the leading note. The ninth is not suitable in the V–VI interrupted cadence. Why not?

A quick way to find V13 in any key is to play V7 with the fifth at the top, and then alter the fifth to a sixth:

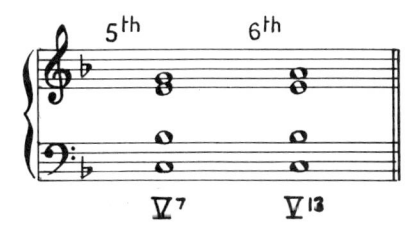

The V13 often appears as an appoggiatura. It may replace the cadential $^6_4$ chord. IIIb is also possible.

(N.B. the doubled third in chord VI in the interrupted cadence.)

Now return to the beginning of the chapter and read through again. Play each quotation and transpose it into at least one other key.

Most of the examples may be sung, and you should arrange with your friends to try them together.

Study this accompaniment written by Cecil Sharp to a folk-song he collected in Somerset (from *Some Lesser Known Folk Songs*, Novello).

Notice the delicate contrast (i) between the flowing style of most of the accompaniment and the short phrases of bars 1, 2 and 9, and (ii) between the stepwise movement in most of the bass line and the fine sweep of bars 4–6.

Point out (i) three examples of chord VI
          (ii) an example of chord III
          (iii) an example of V13
          (iv) an interrupted cadence, V–VI

(v) a plagal cadence, IV–I
   (vi) an imperfect cadence, Ib–V
   (vii) a perfect cadence, V–I
Devise appropriate accompaniments to the following contrasted folk-songs. Sing to your own accompaniments and perform them for your friends.

The Tree in the Valley

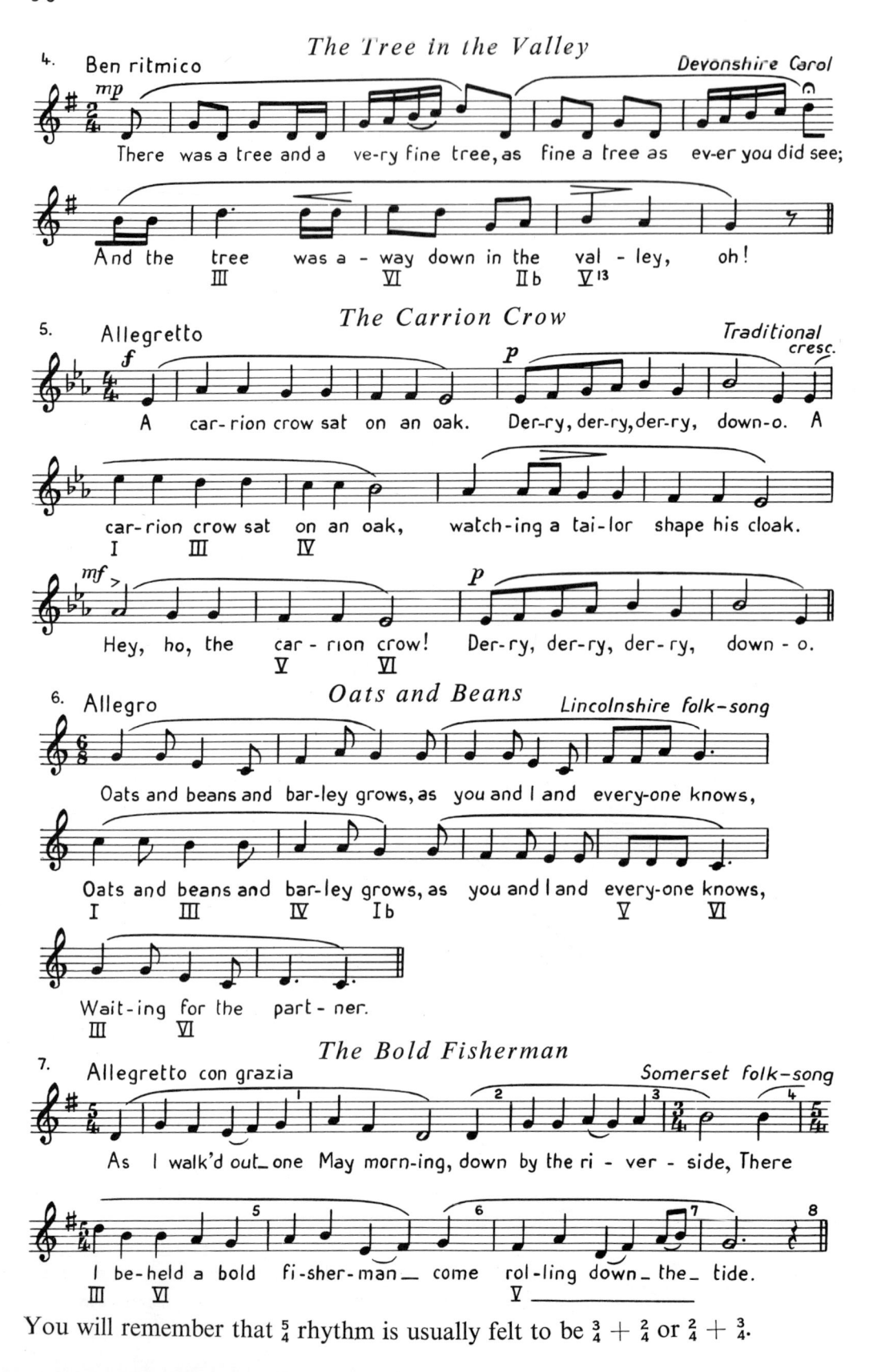

4. Ben ritmico *Devonshire Carol*

There was a tree and a ve-ry fine tree, as fine a tree as ev-er you did see;
And the tree was a-way down in the val - ley, oh!
III   VI   IIb V13

The Carrion Crow

5. Allegretto *Traditional*

A car-rion crow sat on an oak. Der-ry, der-ry, der-ry, down-o. A car-rion crow sat on an oak, watch-ing a tai-lor shape his cloak.
I III IV
Hey, ho, the car-rion crow! Der-ry, der-ry, der-ry, down-o.
V VI

Oats and Beans

6. Allegro *Lincolnshire folk-song*

Oats and beans and bar-ley grows, as you and I and every-one knows,
Oats and beans and bar-ley grows, as you and I and every-one knows,
I III IV Ib V VI
Wait-ing for the part-ner.
III VI

The Bold Fisherman

7. Allegretto con grazia *Somerset folk-song*

As I walk'd out one May morn-ing, down by the ri-ver-side, There I be-held a bold fi-sher-man come rol-ling down the tide.
III VI V

You will remember that $\frac{5}{4}$ rhythm is usually felt to be $\frac{3}{4} + \frac{2}{4}$ or $\frac{2}{4} + \frac{3}{4}$.

Blow Away the Morning Dew

8. Allegro vivace

Up-on the sweet-est sum-mer-time in the mid-dle of the morn, A pret-ty dam-sel I es-pied, the fair-est ev-er born. And sing, blow a-way the morn-ing dew, the dew and the dew, Sing
                                                III   VI
blow a-way the morn-ing dew, how sweet the winds do blow.
   VI   II   Ic

On Christmas Night

9. Flowing and fairly fast   Sussex Carol

On Christ-mas night all Christ-ians sing, to hear the news the an-gels bring. On Christ-mas night all Christ-ians sing, to hear the news the an-gels bring. News of great joy,— news of great mirth, News of our mer-ci-ful King's birth.

Refer back to melodies in previous chapters and experiment with your present harmonic vocabulary.

Decide upon a harmonization of the major scale and learn to play it confidently in every key. We have already given two harmonizations of the descending scale. Here is a suggested harmonization of the ascending form:

I Vb I IV Ib II V7 I

There are many delightful accompaniments in *A European Folk-song Book* by John Horton (Arnold, Leeds) that you would do well to study at this stage.

Add parts for soprano, alto, and tenor:

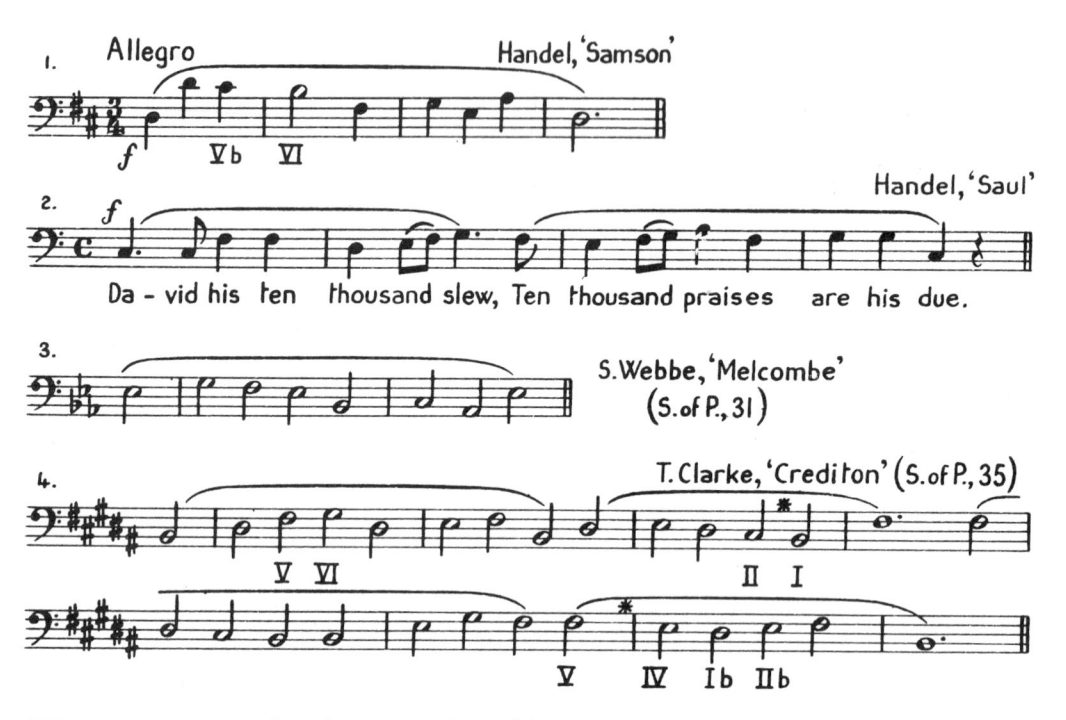

1. Allegro — Handel, 'Samson'

2. Handel, 'Saul'
Da-vid his ten thousand slew, Ten thousand praises are his due.

3. S. Webbe, 'Melcombe' (S. of P., 31)

4. T. Clarke, 'Crediton' (S. of P., 35)

*Use contrary motion between the added parts and the bass.

5. Green's Psalmody (S. of P., 39)

6. Moderately slow — Baring-Gould 'Eudoxia' (S. of P., 49)

7. Majestically — Stuttgart (S. of P., 84)

Add alto, tenor, and bass to these soprano parts.

For further practice, sing and harmonize the tunes in Book I of *The Folk Song Sight Singing Series* (O.U.P.).

CHAPTER EIGHT

INSTRUMENTAL WRITING

Arrangements for Recorders and Percussion

We hope that you are making good use of your developing skill in handling melody and harmony in an interesting way. In this chapter we suggest various creative activities. Whenever possible adapt them to meet the requirements of your group. Transpose settings where necessary to suit the individual voices and instruments. Question the players on the practicability of the parts you write. Devise your own projects in addition to the ones suggested here and be sure that everything that you write is performed, if only to a tiny audience.

Let us suppose that we have been invited to make a three-part arrangement of a folk-song for a group of descant recorder players. They have reached a stage when they can play tunes involving the notes of the scale of C major:

(sounding an 8^{ve} higher)

We decide that 'Old Farmer Buck', transposed into C, would suit our purpose admirably. We sketch in some simple harmonies:

We reflect on the character of our tune. It is lively and humorous, with a touch of mock-pathos in bars 5 and 6. We shall need to devise some rhythmic interest if we are to capture this jauntiness in the added parts. We look at the harmony that we have sketched in and decide that the first bar looks much too staid as it stands. Perhaps we could introduce some movement here by using a first inversion of the tonic chord? We consider the possibility of I–Ib, or Ib–I. If we adopt the former we are faced with an incomplete triad on the third beat of bar I, and again on the first beat of the following bar. But if we begin with the first inversion, we have complete triads on beats one and three, and we notice that the lower parts have the motif of a falling third:

[Musical example a) with three voices I, II, III]

It occurs to us that this falling third is a feature of the tune—see bars 4, 5, 6, and 10. We decide that the idea is worth pursuing. We also reflect that there are possible rhythmic variants of this motif:

[Musical example b), marked *etc.*]

We remind ourselves that it would be tedious and inartistic to persist with a single rhythmic pattern throughout. We consider the effect of ♩ ♩ 𝄾 in bars 1 and 2, and a change to 𝄾 ♩ 𝄾 ♩ in bar 3.

The basic harmonies flow smoothly in bars 2 and 3, so we turn our attention to the cadence at the end of the first phrase. A perfect cadence is obviously called for, but we remember that the opening phrase is repeated and we wonder about the desirability of three perfect cadences in the space of a ten-bar tune. We ponder the possibility of V–VI in place of V–I, and the following progression comes to mind:

[Musical example c)]

This has various features to commend it. It provides movement as the tune stands still; our original idea is developed; the passing notes add a touch of dissonance on the third beat of the bar, and the step-wise movement leads back smoothly to our first inversion chord in bar 1. When bars 1–4 are repeated we shall have the expected perfect cadence:

[musical example d)]

In view of the humour of bars 5 and 6, suggested by the allargando and ensuing presto, together with the use of chords III and VI, we feel that some relaxation of movement is appropriate at this point, and we decide to add a touch of 'bleakness' by omitting the third in chord V.

As we turn our attention to bars 7–10, we feel that a note-for-note repetition of bars 1–4 would be rather dull. We consider the possibility of going above the tune in the final two bars in order to suggest a little climax:

[musical example e)]

This prompts a further thought. Since the arrangement is for a group of players on equal terms, why let one part have the tune throughout—why not share it between the three parts? The final version begins to take shape.

Old Farmer Buck
Arranged for three descant recorders

[musical score for three descant recorders, Allegro]

Choose a folk-song and make an arrangement for a group of your friends to play. Be sure to transpose the melody into a key that is practicable for recorder players.

Valse Noble

Let us now suppose that we wish to make an arrangement of this Schubert waltz for a particular group of school children. We have recorders and percussion at our disposal. The recorder players are not yet capable of playing the Schubert melody, so we decide to retain the piano piece as it stands and write our own parts for recorders and percussion.

Our first task is to examine Schubert's harmony and to make sure that we understand the chords involved.

Next we examine the texture of the music, and we observe certain rhythmic patterns in the underneath parts. For example, in the R.H. of the piano part we find the ♩ ♩ rhythm in almost every bar, and if we imagine the waltz in an orchestral version we realize that the L.H. of the piano part would resolve into two rhythmic figures. We can hear basses and cellos playing the first beats of each bar while the second and third beats are played by violas and second violins.

We decide therefore, to write recorder parts based on the ♩ ♩ rhythm, and to let the percussion instruments have the other rhythms,

♩ 𝄽 𝄽 and 𝄽 ♩ ♩

The waltz is delicate and restrained in feeling, and must not be overloaded in our arrangement. Remember to write recorder parts in such a way that they will sound satisfactory by themselves. Be sure that the percussion parts are not too heavily scored.

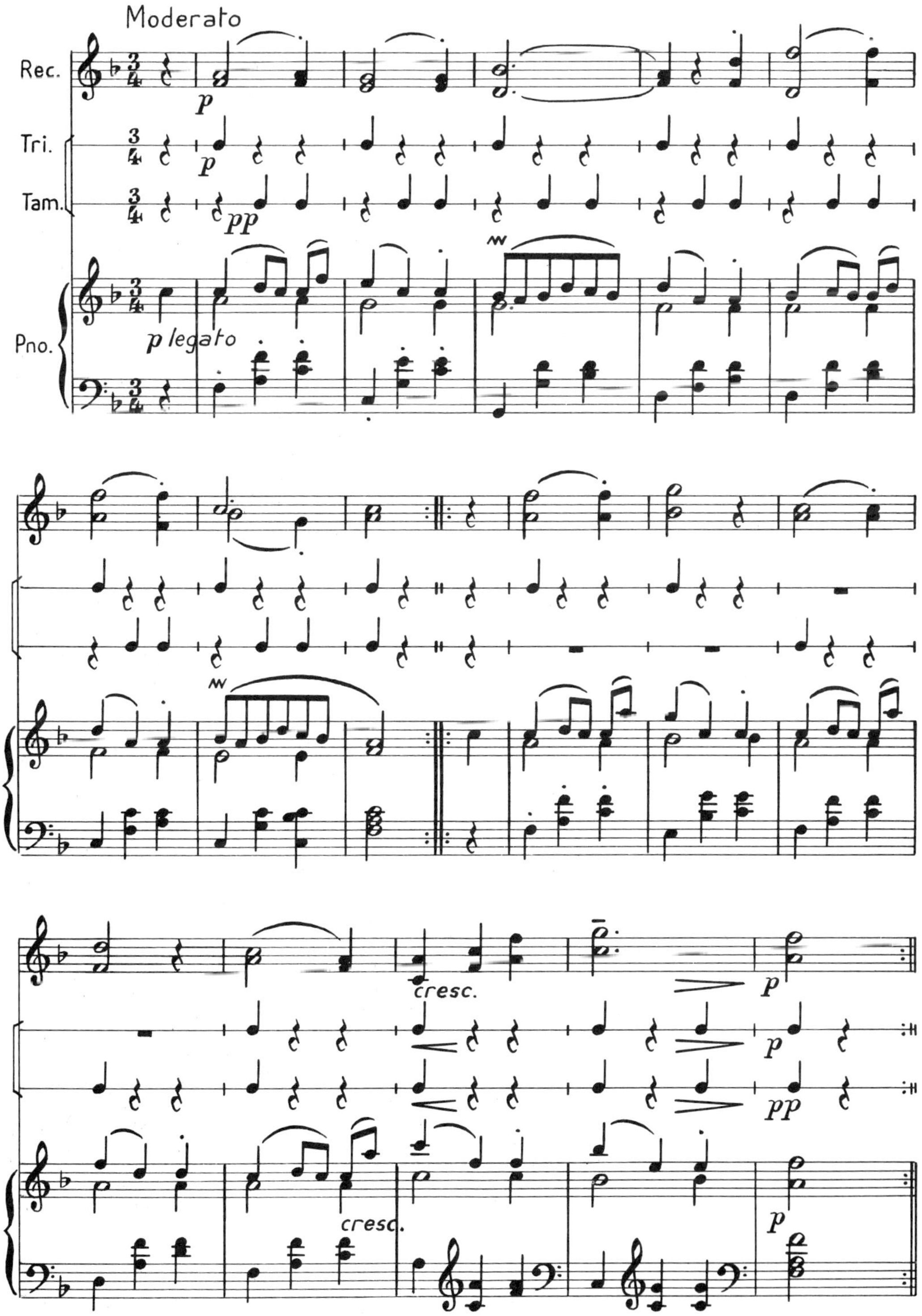
Moderato
Rec.
Tri.
Tam.
Pno.
p
pp
p legato
cresc.
p
pp
cresc.
p

Arrange this dance for piano, recorders, cymbal, and drum:

German Dance

Arrange this melody for three recorders (two trebles and a tenor):

Find out as much as you can about the recorder and its repertoire. Refer to books on fingering and technique.

In the meantime, if you are writing for players of average ability, confine yourself to the easier keys and keep your parts within a limited range—say about an octave and a sixth.

Descant and Tenor
(Tenor sounds as written, Descant sounds an 8ve higher than written)

Treble
(Sounds as written)

Beethoven's 'Ecossaises', the next piece that we ask you to arrange, is rather longer than our usual quotation and so we have inserted a number of rehearsal letters. Such letters are a great help in all concerted music. When a passage needs to be repeated in rehearsal, much time is saved if performers can be directed to a convenient starting point. Make a habit of using these letters in your own scores and parts.

In this particular piece they also serve to draw attention to the form of the music. This is important, because unless you appreciate the form of a piece of music that you are arranging, your scoring is bound to lack something in terms of balance and colour.

Note the following features of the 'Ecossaises':

(a) From the beginning to letter A, one rhythmic pattern persists throughout, ♫ ♩ . The passage is marked 'p'.

(b) Between letters A and B, a new rhythmic pattern appears ♩ ♩ | ♫ ♩ | This is related to the opening pattern, but the extra crotchets introduce an element of vigour and sturdiness. At the same time there is an increase in sonority (note the deep bass notes), together with a exhilarating rise in pitch and a most effective crescendo and diminuendo.

(c) Between letters B and C there is a change of mood. There is more legato phrasing. The melody tends to fall rather than to rise, and the interval of a third is prominent. Again we get a new rhythmic pattern, and again it is based on ingredients that we have already met. (The whole piece is an object lesson on how to get unity and variety from the simplest rhythmic means— ♩, ♫, ♬ .)

(d) The passage from C to the end is a repetition of the bars between A and B. This recapitulation gives the piece balance and shapeliness.

Select a suitable ensemble for your arrangement from the following resources:

Piano, recorders, triangle, tambourine, cymbals, drums, and chime-bars.

We suggest that you might consider reserving certain instruments for exclusive use in one particular section of the piece. Which section do you think we have in mind?

Ecossaises

Allegro — Beethoven

VOCAL WRITING

(i) Two-part writing

Sing these examples and consider the comments.

Allegro — Chorus of slaves — Mozart, 'Magic Flute'

O— lis-ten, what is it that_ tinkles so clear? La-ra-la, la le la-ra-la, la le la-ra-la. 'Tis_ something I ne-ver did see nor did hear, La-ra-la la le la-ra-la, la le la-ra-la.

(∗ = Triangle)

(a) Thirds and sixths are smooth and sweet.

Allegro — Pamina / Papageno

When the magic bells are heard, Chimes of mu-sic wa-king, Wrath for-gets his an-gry_ word, Frowns to smiles are break-ing.

(b) Perfect fifths have a strong, individual flavour. Notice how effective they are at the perfect and imperfect cadences.

(c) Perfect fourths usually arise as appoggiaturas, suspensions or passing notes.

(d) The augmented fourth consists of two leaning notes from the chord of the dominant seventh. (Which key is Mozart using here?)
(e) The passing note (D) forms a major second with the harmony note (C). Such a dissonance would be more noticeable at a slow tempo.

There is no need for the two voices to sing together all the time:

The First Witch is silent while the Second Witch echoes her words and rhythm. They then combine together in thirds beginning with a syncopation. After the previous jerky, broken style, the longer chord and the thirds are very expressive.

Melodic intervals, as well as words and rhythm, may be imitated:

The Second Soprano sings a two-bar phrase that is imitated exactly by the First Soprano. Next, a shorter phrase is sung four times, the entries of the two voices overlapping, and the harmony being restricted to one chord. Such exact imitation is attractive for a short time but would soon grow tedious. In the following bars the melodic imitation is approximate, changes of harmony become more frequent, and the use of suspensions, auxiliary notes and passing notes bring urgency into the style and combine to drive the music on to a convincing cadence.

In this style, the bass of the instrumental accompaniment is usually independent of the voice parts, i.e., it does not move in consecutive unisons, octaves or fifths with any one voice. The upper instruments, however, frequently support the voices by playing with them in unison or octaves. Comment upon this further quotation from Handel.

Andante
Handel, 'Judas Maccabaeus'
mp
Come, e - ver- smi - ling li-ber-ty, come, smi-ling li-ber-ty,
mp
Come, e - ver- smi - ling li-ber-ty, smi-ling li-ber-ty,
p
1 2 3 4
And with thee bring thy jocund train, with — thee bring thy
And with thee bring thy jocund train, with thee bring thy
5 6 7
jo - cund train.
jo - cund train.
8

Which of the imitations are exact?
Which interval does the composer most favour (a) in the melody?
(b) in the harmony?
Analyse the harmony. Is the rate of chord change steady?
What is a little unusual about the first chord in bar 5?
With which cadence does this extract conclude?
Which of the two quotations from Handel do you find the more interesting?

Complete the following and compare your solutions with those of the composers.

1. Complete for two sopranos.

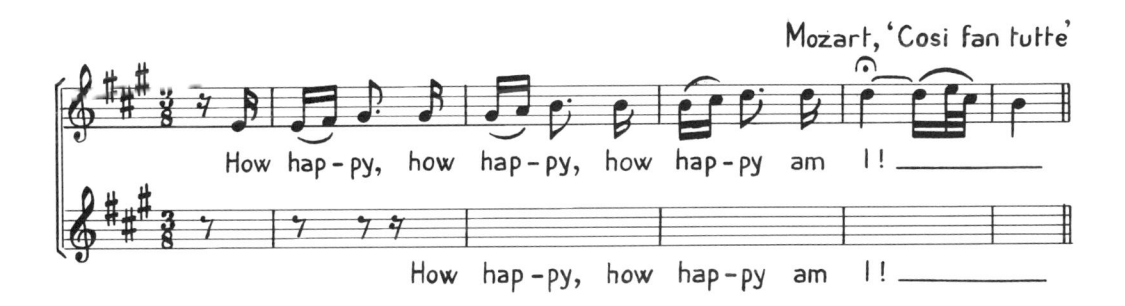

Mozart, 'Cosi fan tutte'

How hap-py, how hap-py, how hap-py am I!

How hap-py, how hap-py am I!

2. Complete for two sopranos.

Moderato — Morley

It was a lo-ver and his lass, with a hey, with a ho, with a

It — was

hey   no ni   no, and a hey — no ni no, ni no.

with a hey, with a   ho, — with a   hey no ni no, ni no.

3. Complete for tenor, bass, and piano.

Mozart, 'Cosi fan tutte'

4. Continue the canon in the alto and then complete the simple continuo part in quavers. What is the connection between the words and the form of the music?

[Musical excerpt: Bach, Mass in B minor — Andante, marked p. Soprano and Alto enter imitatively with the text "Et in unum, in unum Do— — — — —minum," accompanied by Strings and harpsichord continuo.]

(ii) Three and four-part writing

Imitative counterpoint and sturdy homophony are well contrasted in this extract from *The Christmas Story*.

Analyse the harmony.
   How many points of imitation are there?
   Comment on the intervals between the voices.
   Point out (a) an imperfect cadence
             (b) a plagal cadence
             (c) a syncopation
   How far is the bass part in the orchestra independent of the voices?
   Which imitations are exact?

Notice that the harmonic progression is strong and steady. It is difficult to write lucid counterpoint over a rapidly changing chordal basis.

The rests help to avoid the congestion that might easily arise when several voices and instruments are involved together.

Sing and compare the following extracts.

a) Menotti, 'Amahl'

b) Allegretto con grazia — Menotti, 'Amahl'

Shep-herds: E-mi-ly, E-mi-ly, Michael, Bartholomew, how are your children and

how are your sheep? Do-ro-thy, Do-ro-thy, Pe-ter, E - van-ge-line,
give me your hand, come a-long _ with me All the children have
mumps. All the flocks are a-sleep, We are going with A -
- mahl, bring - ing gifts to the Kings.

c) Allegretto — Menotti, 'Amahl'

p staccatissimo

SHEPHERDS

O-lives and quin-ces, ap-ples and rai-sins, nut-meg and myr-tle, medlars and chest-nuts, this is all we she-herds can of-fer you.

122

Allegro moderato — Gustav Holst, Psalm CXLVIII

123

Which of the examples are homophonic and which contrapuntal?
Are thirds and sixths always the intervals used consecutively?
Which parts are doubled?
Point out syncopations. Comment on other aspects of the rhythms, particularly the less usual.
By what technical means have the composers so brilliantly matched the words and the music?

The following quotations are taken from well-known and easily-obtainable scores.

Complete the missing parts, taking care in each case to maintain the style, and then compare your working with the original. You may occasionally consider some detail of your working to be equally as good, or better, than that of the composer: in such an event take the two manuscripts to your tutor and ask for his opinion.

p
shepherds, shepherds be; How merrily we live
that shep – herds be; How merrily we live
p
live that How merrily we
mp
that shepherds be, that shepherds be. Roundelays, rounde-
mp
that shepherds be, that shepherds be. Rounde-
live that shepherds be, that shep – herds be.
– lays, roundelays, rounde – lays. roundelays, still we
– lays, roundelays, rounde – lays, roundelays, rounde-lays, still we
Roundelays, rounde-lays, roundelays, still we
mf
sing with mer-ry glee, roundelays, still we sing with mer-ry glee.
mf
sing with mer-ry glee, roundelays, still we sing with mer-ry glee.
mf
sing with mer – ry glee, still we sing with mer – ry glee.

3. **Allegro** — from 'The Beggars' Opera' (1728)

Tenor: Fill ev'ry glass, for wine in-spires us and fires us with cou-rage love and joy.

Tenor: Fill ev'ry glass, for wine in-spires us with love and joy.

Bass: Fill ev'ry glass, for wine in-spires us with cou-rage love and joy.

4. **Allegro**

Tenor: (vocalise)

Tenor: Let us

Bass: Let us take the road! Hark! I hear the sound of coach-es! The hour of at-tack ap-proach-es, T'your arms, brave boys, and load!

5.

Allegretto leggiero

Youth's the sea-son made for joys, Love is then our du-ty;
Youth's the sea-son made for joys, Love is then our du-ty;
Youth's the sea-son made for joys, Love is then our du-ty;

She a-lone who that em-ploys, Well de-serves her beau-ty.

Let's
Let's be gay, While we may, Beauty's a flower des-pis'd in de-cay.
Let's be gay, While we may, Beauty's des-pis'd in de-cay.

Youth's the sea-son made for joys, Love is then our du-ty.

128

6. Andante — Schütz, St. Matthew Passion

Write parts for alto and tenor in a more homophonic style:

7. Adagio

Thanks be to our Lord, Thanks be to our Lord, to Je - sus Christ.

8. Allegro

Handel, 'Messiah'

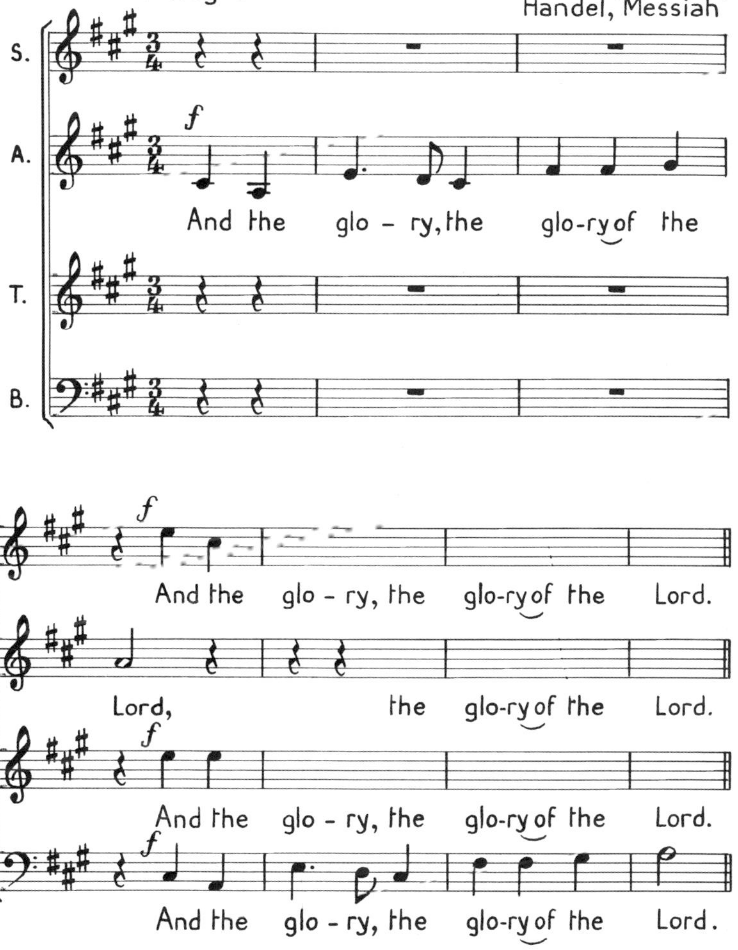

9. Allegro

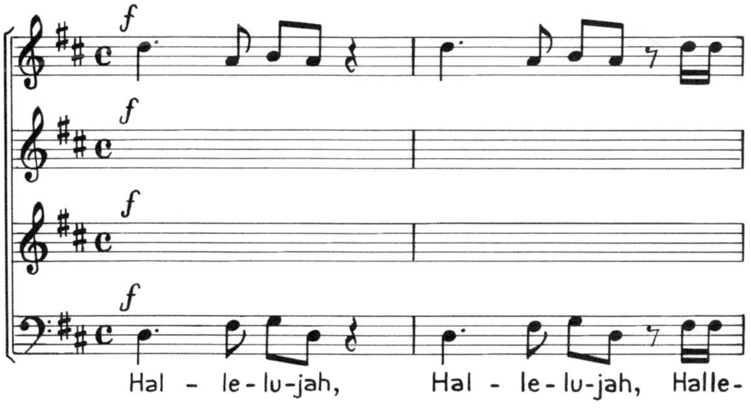

-lu-jah, Halle-lu-jah, Hal - le - lu-jah!

(iii) Solo, chorus, and accompaniment

In previous chapters we have suggested introducing vocal harmonizations in chorus songs. We now combine this with instrumental accompaniment.

Sing and play these two settings:

In waltz country dance style

Solo
And it's blow the man down, bul-lies, blow the man down.

Chorus
Way, ——— ay ——— blow the man down.

Blow the man down, bul-lies, blow the man down. Oh give us some breath to blow the man down.

Eagerly
mp
Recorder
mp
Drum
Solo
mf
Voices
Hark, now the drums beat up a-gain, For all true sol-diers, gen-tle-men, Then let us list and march, I say, O-ver the hills and
Piano
mp
rit. . . .
a tempo
rit. . . .
a tempo

far a-way. O'er the hills and o'er the main, To Flan-ders, Por-tu-gal and Spain, Queen Anne com-mands and

Discuss the settings above and consider these points:

    (a) The more instruments and voices involved, the more likely are there to be a great many rests in the score. Choose your instruments carefully and remember they often have more effect if used for part of the song only.

    (b) You may often prefer to write in 3 vocal parts. A chorus in 3-part harmony is fuller and usually more satisfactory than one in 2 parts. It can often be sung, with appropriate transposition, almost equally well by a mixed group (SAB), a group of girls (SSA), or a group of men (TTB).

Improvise pianoforte accompaniments for the songs following. Write and sing arrangements of the choruses for 2, 3, or 4 parts as you think appropriate, and add parts for additional instruments if the performance may be improved thereby.

Ravenscroft, Deuteromelia, 1609

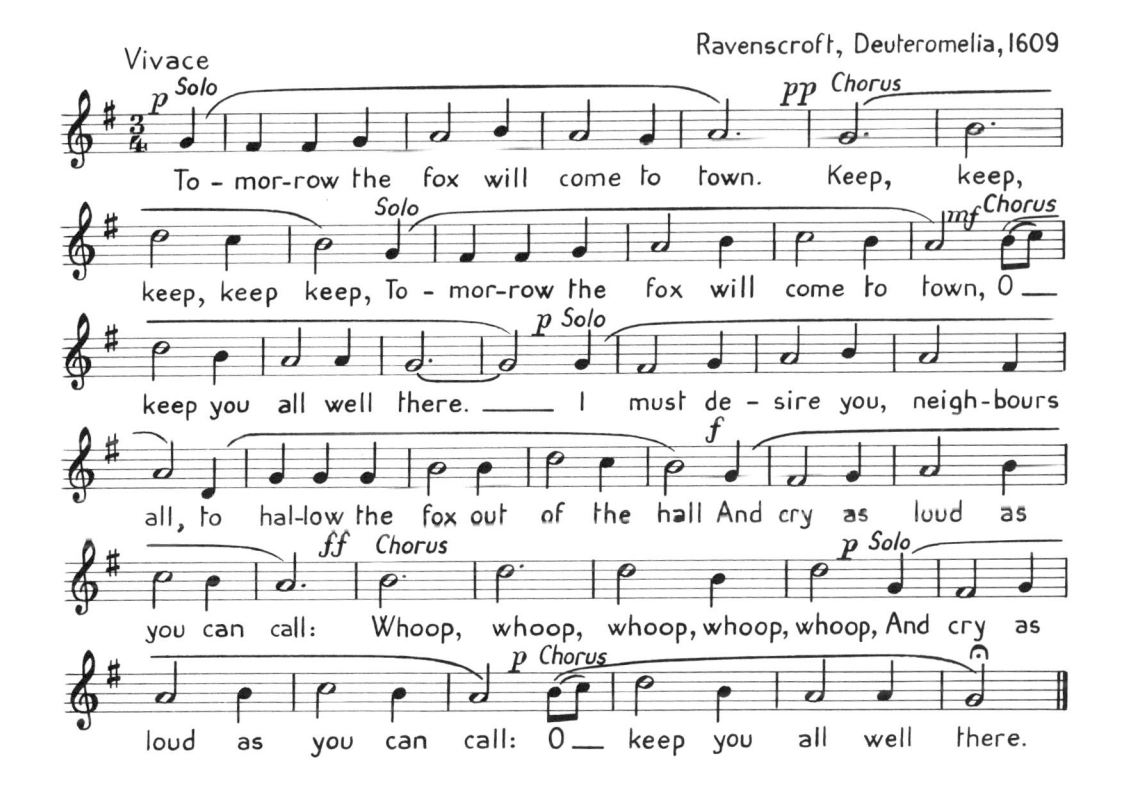

Vivace

To-morrow the fox will come to town. Keep, keep, keep, keep keep, To-morrow the fox will come to town, O— keep you all well there.— I must de-sire you, neigh-bours all, to hal-low the fox out of the hall And cry as loud as you can call: Whoop, whoop, whoop, whoop, whoop, And cry as loud as you can call: O— keep you all well there.

2. He'll steal the cock out from his flock, etc.
3. He'll steal the hen out of the pen,
4. He'll steal the duck out of the brook,
5. He'll steal the lamb e'en from his dam.

Be alive to the swift tempo and exciting dynamics. Keep the texture light and simple.

2. *Joggingly*

Were you e-ver in Que-bec Stow-ing tim-ber on the deck? Where there's a King with a gol-den crown Ri-ding on a don-key. Hey! ho! a-way we go Don-key ri-ding, don-key ri-ding, Hey! ho! a-way we go Ri-ding on a don-key.

2 Were you ever off the Horn
  Where it's always fine and warm,
  And seen the lion and the unicorn
    Riding on a donkey?
    Hey! ho! etc.

3 Were you ever in Cardiff Bay?
  Where the folks all shout 'Hooray!
  Here comes Johnny with his three months pay
    Riding on a donkey!'
    Hey! ho! etc.

Consider the possibility of the voices dividing 'subito *ff*' on 'Hooray ...' in the last verse.

3. Robustly

English Sea Song

Chorus

We'll rant and we'll roar like true British sail-ors, We'll range and we'll roam o'er all the salt seas, Un-til we strike sound-ings in the Chan-nel of old Eng-land. From U-shant to Scil-ly is thir-ty five leagues.

4. Jovially

from Playford's Pleasant Musical Companion, Part II 1687

mf Solo

Sir Eg-la-more that va-liant knight, Fa-la-lan-key down dil-ly. He took up his sword and he went to fight, Fa-la-lan-key down dil-ly. And as he rode o'er hill and dale, All arm-éd in a shirt of mail Fa-la-la la-la, Fa-la-lan-key down dil-ly.

5. **Con spirito** — Sussex Folk-Song

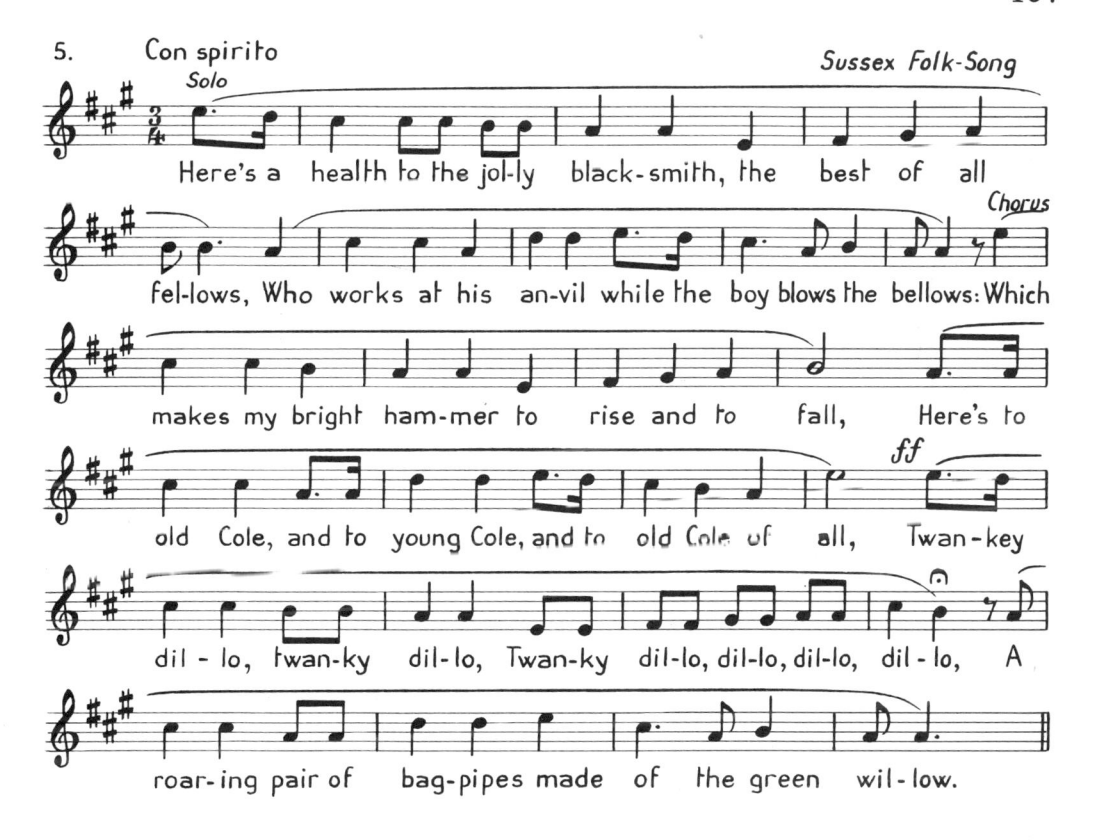

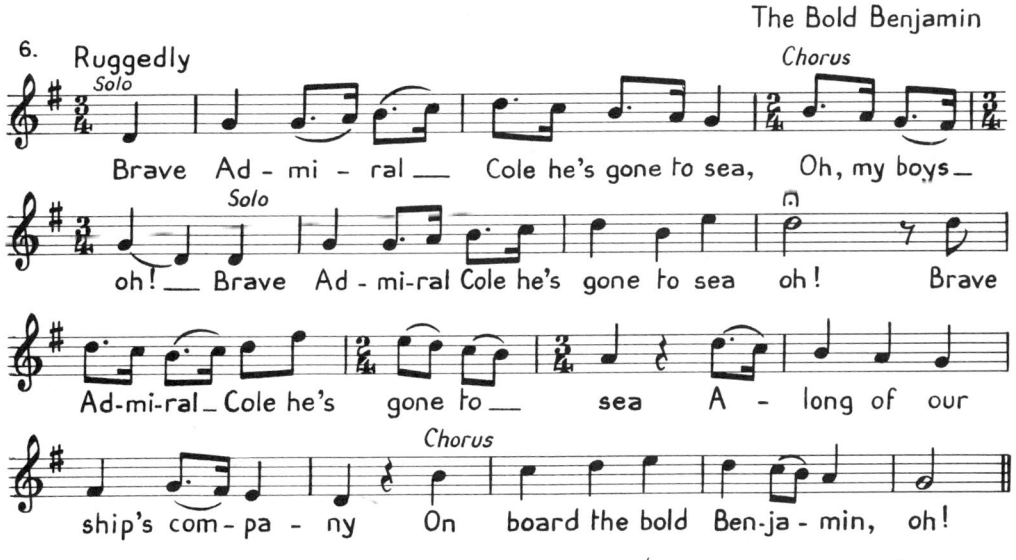

Solo: Here's a health to the jolly blacksmith, the best of all fellows, Who works at his anvil while the boy blows the bellows: *Chorus:* Which makes my bright hammer to rise and to fall, Here's to old Cole, and to young Cole, and to old Cole of all, Twankey dillo, twanky dillo, Twanky dillo, dillo, dillo, dillo, A roaring pair of bagpipes made of the green willow.

6. **Ruggedly** — The Bold Benjamin

Solo: Brave Admiral Cole he's gone to sea, *Chorus:* Oh, my boys oh! *Solo:* Brave Admiral Cole he's gone to sea oh! Brave Admiral Cole he's gone to sea A-long of our ship's company *Chorus:* On board the bold Benjamin, oh!

Four more verses of this Dorset song may be found in 'The Penguin Book of English Folk Songs'

You have now sung, played and arranged a good many tunes in the major mode. Our last quotation forms a bridge to Book Two, in which we discuss other forms of scale. Experiment at the piano with the harmonization of this beautiful song which Vaughan Williams quotes in his opera *Hugh the Drover*.